Praise for *Design* ...

'Enlightening. Inspiring.'
–Fiona Capp, *The Age*

'Deceptively easy to read ... Full of profound ideas and revelations.'
–Madeleine Swain, *Architectural Review*

'Page and Memmott have given us a profoundly important vision for Australian design, one that has tapped into ancient conversations about the human connection to nature, and how the built environment can play a vital part in this dialogue. With respect for Country at its core, they tell us about their own adventures in reprising thousands of years of wisdom and Indigenous understanding of this world from elders: not a replica of a world thousands of kilometres away in the northern hemisphere, but the one the ancestors sang into existence here. Their contributions can make Australia truly a home in concert with its environments and climate, designed to reconnect us to Country and our ecological responsibility to care for it.'
—Marcia Langton AO

'A major step forward in providing a deeper understanding for all Australians of what "Country" is: that everything is part of the same continuum – nature, land, sea, sky and humans – including what is designed and built. Design and architecture are not nouns, they are verbs.

'There is no better time to learn these lessons. The injunction to tread lightly upon the earth, to understand Country and its knowledge, has never been more important.'
—Lucy Turnbull AO

DESIGN

Aboriginal and Torres Strait Islander peoples are advised that this book contains the names and images of people who have passed away.

The stories in this book are shared with the permission of the original storytellers.

DESIGN

Building on Country

ALISON PAGE &
PAUL MEMMOTT

Thames & Hudson | national museum australia

First published in Australia in 2021
by Thames & Hudson Australia Pty Ltd
11 Central Boulevard, Portside Business Park
Port Melbourne, Victoria 3207
ABN: 72 004 751 964

thamesandhudson.com.au

Design © Thames & Hudson Australia 2021

Introduction © Margo Neale/NMA 2021
Text © Alison Page and Paul Memmott 2021
Images © copyright remains with the individual copyright holders

24 23   5 4

Thames & Hudson Australia wishes to acknowledge that Aboriginal and Torres Strait Islander
people are the first storytellers of this nation and the traditional custodians of the land on which
we live and work. We acknowledge their continuing culture and pay respect to Elders past, present
and future.

Thames & Hudson Australia thanks Professor Lynette Russell AM, ARC Kathleen Fitzpatrick
Laureate Fellow, Monash Indigenous Studies Centre, for providing editorial advice.

978 1 76076 140 0 (paperback)
978 1 76076 185 1 (ebook)

A catalogue record for this
book is available from the
National Library of Australia

Every effort has been made to trace accurate ownership of copyrighted text and visual materials
used in this book. Errors or omissions will be corrected in subsequent editions, provided
notification is sent to the publisher.

This project has been assisted by the Australian Government through
the Australia Council, its arts funding and advisory body.

First Knowledges is a series that complements the National Museum of Australia's Clever Country
online videos.

Front and inside cover: *Layers of the Land* by Alison Page

Series editor: Margo Neale
Cover design: Nada Backovic
Typesetting: Megan Ellis
Printed and bound in Australia by McPherson's Printing Group

*To the Aboriginal Old People who taught us about Country
and their first knowledges; and to the new generation of design
practitioners – both Aboriginal and non-Aboriginal – who choose
to apply these knowledges, taking Australia into a better and
sustainable future.*

NOTE ON SPELLING

Readers may note that for different language groups, variant spellings occur for similar words, cultural groups or names.

DESIGN TERMS USED IN THIS BOOK

barkuwen	large two-handled Lardil dugong net
dulnhu kirra	Lardil grass-string net used for catching dulnhu fish
dulnhul	Lardil net for catching fish in runs in channels and gutters
dumunthar	Lardil elliptical scoop net
gunya	traditional house (widespread term)
jadiyeli	Kaiadilt throwing stick made from a *Terminalia* species (*dankaburrd*)
kalwa	Bardi double raft
kujiji	specialised Kaiadilt hunting spear
kurrumbu	Lardil pronged fishing spear (the Kaiadilt name for this spear is similar, being *kurumbu*)
mijil	Lardil hand-net or purse-net
murruku	Lardil spearthrower
muurraj	Kaiadilt hunting spear
nawi	Eora traditional bark canoe
ngampirr	Lardil enclosed wet-weather shelter
ngunnhu	fish trap in Barwon River at Brewarrina
ngurruwarra	Kaiadilt rock-wall fish trap
wungkurr	Lardil windbreak

CONTENTS

FIRST KNOWLEDGES

MARGO NEALE, SERIES EDITOR

In the Aboriginal worldview, everything starts and ends with Country. Yet there are no beginnings in this worldview, nor are there any endings. Everything is part of a continuum, an endless flow of life and ideas emanating from Country, which is often referred to as the Dreaming.

In the Dreaming, as in Country, there is no division between the animate and inanimate. Everything is living: people, animals, plants, rocks, earth, water and air. Creator ancestors created the Country and its interface, the Dreaming. In turn, Dreaming speaks for Country, which holds the Law and knowledge. Country has Dreaming; Country is Dreaming. It is this oneness of all things that explains how and why Aboriginal knowledges belong to an integrated system of learning, which you will encounter throughout the First Knowledges series.

Design: Building on Country by Alison Page and Paul Memmott, the second book in the series, takes us deep into Country and shows how it is a way of seeing and relating to the world, where there is no separation between people and nature. It demonstrates how Indigenous people think of Country as they would a family member: how we yearn for Country and call to it. The earth is our mother. We belong to Country; it does not belong to us.

Country includes the built environment and objects, which reflect both a conceptual and a physical process with ancestral and cultural dimensions. Traditionally, structures were made from 'Country' and, as temporary structures, were absorbed back into Country after use. Country, in combination with climatic conditions (which are also expressions of Country), determined the style and nature of the structures that humans built and adapted to their needs. Thus the built environment and Country formed an integrated cultural landscape.

Country is the wellspring from which all knowledge originates. It holds information, innovations, stories and secrets – from medicine, engineering, ecology and astronomy to social mores on how to live, and social organisation, including moiety division and kinship systems. If Country holds all knowledge, then Country is clever – thus the title of the National Museum of Australia's *Clever Country* online films, produced by Alison Page and Nik Lachajczak, that complement the First Knowledges books. These aim to give readers an in-depth understanding of Indigenous expertise in six areas: Songlines; architecture, engineering and design; land management and future farms; plants; astronomy; and innovation.

Book 1 in the First Knowledges series, *Songlines: The Power and Promise*, is foundational to the series, just as Songlines are foundational to our culture – to what we know, how we know it and when we know it. Songlines are our library, our archive from which all subjects are derived, including the knowledge of the design, orientation and siting of our built structures, as well as the design of objects such as boomerangs and fish traps, with their ancestral dimension. In this book you will learn how objects can be imbued with a spirit and a soul, and have a kinship connection to living people and ancestors. In Indigenous cultures, the matter of objects is alive with energies.

To date, little accessible material has been available on Indigenous knowledges for general readers. We hope this series goes some way to bridging that gap. Furthermore, these books introduce the knowledges of First Australians in ways that are in line with Indigenous ways of knowing and being, and overturn outdated ways of representing – or misrepresenting – Aboriginal and Torres Strait Islander peoples. Throughout the series, we acknowledge expertise from both Aboriginal and Western disciplines. This form of co-authorship is in the spirit of reconciliation, working well together interculturally. Here, Alison writes from an Indigenous perspective on her areas of expertise: design and storytelling; while Paul writes from a Western perspective on his areas of expertise: anthropology and architecture. Both authors are pioneers in their respective fields and are working with these knowledges primarily through a contemporary rather than a historical lens. Their cultural and individual differences are one of the strengths of this book.

Some prevailing assumptions about our culture will be challenged and discussed in the First Knowledges series, such as that Aboriginal people were only hunters and gatherers, not farmers; that fire is destructive, not a tool for managing the land; that we did not build houses and had no technology, no knowledge system and no history, only myths and legends; that we had no scientists, doctors or lawyers; that we were incapable of innovation. In truth, if we did not have a long history as innovators, we could not

3

have adapted to immense climatic changes, including an ice age and rapid sea-level rise, pestilence and colonisation. And we are still here.

While it is well known that colonialism has had an enormous impact on Indigenous societies, this book reveals the other side of that coin: the significant influences that Aboriginal and Torres Strait Islander cultures have had on Australian society and history, and the important contribution they are making, which in many ways mainstream Australia is only beginning to recognise. In the process of conveying profound insights into the traditional knowledges of the First Australians, Alison and Paul illuminate a new way forward, a Country-focused approach that could define a unique Australian design identity – one that truly responds to the ebb and flow of Country and is powered by some very old ideas to reinvigorate those ancient conversations about the human connection to nature, and how the built environment can play a vital part in this dialogue. They offer a transformational perspective for Australian designers, architects and engineers: to be part of a design ethos that views the construction of the built environment as an extension of Country and incorporates creation stories and ancestral connections for all cultural groups. Buildings can become story places that connect with each other, much like Songlines reaching across the continent.

The English language can't effectively describe the many new ideas you will encounter in the First Knowledges series, but we hope the concepts in the books will inspire you to learn and expand your worldview to encompass limitless other possibilities, including ways in which you can learn from the Aboriginal archive of knowledge embodied in Country.

1

PERSONAL PERSPECTIVES

ALISON PAGE

Hedonism was all the rage in 1996 when I was a third-year design student. Sustainability and socially responsible principles were a mere whisper on campus. The idea that meaningful stories would drive design decisions was dismissed. Everything was form and aesthetic, and it was all rather depressing.

My major assignment was yet another restaurant design, and I wondered how long it would last if it were ever built. The refitting of spaces for retail and hospitality was only ever supposed to have a life cycle of seven years, after which the materials were destined for landfill. I felt I had made a dreadful mistake signing up to be an interior designer in an increasingly wasteful and materialistic world.

I wasn't alone. Years before, architect Robin Boyd had called the Australian identity 'second-hand American' and described our obsession with pasting imported woods over native boards a scourge of 'featurism'.[1] Featurism epitomised the Australian disconnection from nature, whether it was the cutting-down of trees to install a drain or the adoption of materials with no regard to the landscape or climate. The materials in high rotation when I was studying were far worse than the veneers that Boyd spoke of: medium-density fibreboard, for example, was a composite board that was banned in most countries because of its heavy levels of cancerous formaldehyde and lots and lots of plastic.

I felt a widening tension between the socially conscious Indigenous woman that I was becoming and my work as a designer of decorated spaces for eating and drinking. This changed when one of my lecturers, George Verghese, asked whether I had heard of 'Aboriginal architecture'. He was referring to his homeland of Canada, where architects such as Douglas Cardinal were bringing their Indigenous storytelling and values to the built environment and creating deeply meaningful places. When I heard those two words, 'Aboriginal' and 'architecture', put together for the first time, the universe expanded in an instant. Nothing would be the same for me again, thankfully.

As soon as I graduated, I forced my way into a job at the New South Wales Government Architect's office, which in 1995 had established Australia's first Aboriginal architecture group, Merrima

Design. I had met Indigenous architects Dillon Kombumerri, a descendant of the Yugambeh people of the Gold Coast, and Kevin O'Brien, a descendant of the Kaurareg and Meriam people of north-eastern Australia, a year before and I was desperate to join them.

I first encountered Kevin and Dillon when they were outspoken audience members at an engineering forum. During a presentation about Aboriginal housing in the Western Desert, Kevin stood up and yelled that he would rather live in a gunya (traditional house) any day. His point was that the problems of Aboriginal housing had been getting worse year after year, and that Indigenous people often erected traditional structures outside contemporary houses and had extension cords running inside, reducing the 'normal house' to a large power box. I had seen excellent examples of tarted-up gunyas at Oak Valley, near Maralinga, with stereos, lounges, fridges and televisions stuffed into these ephemeral structures, which were much better designed to withstand the extreme temperature fluctuations in the Great Victoria Desert than government housing was.

It was refreshing to see Indigenous architects commenting on what they thought was culturally appropriate: at the time, it was revolutionary. So as soon as I graduated, I walked into the office of the Government Architect and demanded a job, arguing that in order to deliver appropriate design services to communities, they needed a woman on their team.

Luckily for me, I was hired. The years that followed were probably some of the most fertile of my career in terms of forming and developing an approach to contemporary design. With mentors like my co-author of this book, Paul Memmott, and Rick Leplastrier and Glenn Murcutt, I spent many hours pondering how the built environment could be an extension of Country. Seeds that were sown all those years ago are now taking root and have become foundational to the way that all of us practise design.

In 1999, the three of us from Merrima travelled to the Hawkesbury River for an architecture-student camp to demonstrate what Sydney would have been like before colonisation. It was there that we started talking about how the layers of the built environment could build either 'on country' or 'on Country'. This distinction encapsulates my journey into Indigenous knowledges. I gleaned information from books in the library, pieced things together from conversations with elders and mentors, and learnt from making many mistakes and from hours and hours of reflecting.

As a 'concrete Koori', I am a typical urban Aboriginal who has not had the privilege of sitting under a tree with my aunties to learn the ways of my people via the oral traditions for which our culture is renowned. My people are from La Perouse at Captain Cook's landing place in south-east Sydney: ground zero for the colonial destruction of our Indigenous cultures. My family were blue-collar workers on the wharves, in chemical plants and in trades. Through design, I have discovered my own identity as well as our traditional knowledges, which are an endless puzzle for me. I have only started making connections, but with more collaborations – including on this book with Paul – I will discover a few more pieces; and with age, I just might start designing my own puzzle pieces to fill the gaps.

PAUL MEMMOTT

My journey has to start with acknowledging the many Aboriginal Old People who taught me, passed on their knowledge and encouraged me to use it appropriately in my teaching. It is of high priority for me now to find ways to pass this on again to young Aboriginal and non-Aboriginal people. I try in this book to respectfully share a little about the most influential of my old teachers – in particular, my Lardil and Kaiadilt mentors from the Wellesley Islands, and Alyawarr elders from Central Australia – who lived a traditional lifestyle in the early decades of the 20th century. I've tried to understand the significance of the teachings of these elders throughout my life, but any deficiencies are my own fault.

I have had an unusual intertwined career as an anthropologist, architect and university researcher. As an anthropologist I was led into Aboriginal ethnography, material culture, social organisation, kinship and land tenure, and then into consultancy on land claims in the Northern Territory in the 1980s and native title claims in a number of states during the 1990s. This extended to a range of pressing social issues and associated teaching and consultancy challenges, such as historical transparency, deaths in custody, family violence, intergenerational trauma, homelessness and identity erosion. I have aimed to apply my understanding of these problems in the workshops I've been invited to run by the Myuma Group at the Dugalunji Camp in Camooweal in outback Queensland over the past fourteen years. Young Aboriginal adults (and Torres Strait Islanders at times, too) undertake pre-vocational training in these workshops to understand their family and tribal histories and strengthen their self-confidence about who they are and where they come from, as they step into employment.

The parallel strand of architecture led me into Western design disciplines, and then into Aboriginal housing in the early 1970s and culturally appropriate housing design. By the 1990s, I was working on the challenging problem of how to reform institutional architecture – prisons, courthouses, mental health facilities, schools, hospitals, clinics and aged care homes – in a culturally appropriate way for Aboriginal people. How to make safe places!

Today there is an increasingly loud call for culturally appropriate environments for Indigenous people, but little tried and proven knowledge about how to achieve them. This enormous task falls to the lot of younger designers as the values of Australian society gradually change. When I was an undergraduate, there was minimal recognition of Aboriginal architecture or design apart from some rock art and Albert Namatjira's paintings. Today, some of the biggest design firms in Australia request consultancy advice on how to incorporate references to local Aboriginal cultures into their work.

Part of my role in the 1990s was to teach and nurture the first generation of Aboriginal architects with my soulmate and colleague, the late Col James from the University of Sydney. Australia was a generation behind New Zealand, the USA and Canada in pushing for Indigenous inclusivity in design professionalism. One of the most rewarding experiences of my later career has been to see the forging of an international network of Indigenous designers and architects.

Likewise, writing this book has involved a thoroughly enjoyable partnership with my co-author, Alison Page – bonding and stimulating and building off one another – and an appreciated opportunity for team creativity. Importantly, it has enabled me to pass on the knowledge I received from the Old People of this ancient continent to a younger generation of Aboriginal designers and authors. The result has strengthened our combined contribution to *Design: Building on Country* for the next generations.

Bara, bulub, bokman: Looking for 'design'

When we started this book, I brainstormed the idea of having an Aboriginal word meaning 'design' as the title. This raised a number of problems. The first was finding such a word. The second was choosing which language: although most of the original 360 or so Aboriginal languages, many with different dialects, have sadly ceased to be spoken, there are still several hundred wordlists and dictionaries.[2] The third problem was how to create a broad book on Aboriginal design with examples covering a range of language groups but a title in only one language. I'd tried to resolve this issue before with my Aboriginal architecture book titled *Gunyah, Goondie + Wurley*.[3]

I contacted a linguist colleague, Dr Erich Round, who serendipitously informed me that he was developing a tool for exploring a large number of written Aboriginal-language dictionaries, to locate words with similar meanings. He sent me an index of English translations that took over an hour to peruse, as there were about 4000 of them. The list certainly didn't contain the word 'design': clearly it didn't easily translate, on a word-to-word basis, into any Aboriginal language. From the list, however, I selected a set of keywords comprising the closest synonyms I could find: become, bring forth, compose, decorate, imagine, integrate, intuit, make, manufacture, originate, put together, shape up.

These words were fed back into the program and about 320 words were identified in numerous Aboriginal languages from all over Australia. Most were verbs indicating some active process. Although some were generic, others were tied to particular products or outcomes – for example, an object chiselled from timber, or making a sound like thunder. 'Make' was the most common correlation with 'design', but many senses of 'make' seemed to mean 'the manufacturing of a regularly made object using a longstanding known tradition of process and product' and few could be interpreted as making a new or novel design. However, a number prescribed mixing ingredients in particular ways to create something that could be either new or according to a recipe, as in cooking creations. Three words initially jumped out for possible combination to encompass this range: *bara*, *bulub* and *bokman*, drawn from the Gangulu, Bilinarra and Djambarrpuyngu languages respectively. If we had gone ahead with these words as a book title, the next step would have been to understand them in more detail and get permission from the language groups to use their words in this way.

In the end, we decided upon 'Design' (in English) as the title for the book. An English dictionary would typically define 'design' as a plan for making an object or system, or for carrying out a specific activity as a process, and this definition would include the types of meanings I have listed that cover Aboriginal designing. However, there is more to Aboriginal design than this, in that certain designs have come from the Dreaming and are founded on a profound understanding of 'being on Country'.

2

OBJECTS AND SPIRITUALITY: BUILDING ON COUNTRY

ALISON PAGE

Bennelong Point, the site of Australia's most recognisable building, the Sydney Opera House, was known by the traditional owners of the land as Tu-bow-gule, meaning 'where the knowledge waters meet'. What was the knowledge held here at the confluence of the saltwater and freshwater where the Tank Stream meets the ocean?

The site was home to extensive middens, said to be up to 12 metres high, which is testament to the abundance and variety of seafood in the area. After the arrival of the First Fleet in 1788, this place was taken over for cattle and renamed Cattle Point. Then, as construction started on the buildings on Macquarie Street, the middens were repurposed into a lime slurry to form the buildings' foundations and the place was again renamed, this time as Limeburners' Point.

The knowledge about how to crush the shells and release the lime to bind stone and bricks for building was something that my people practised. I would regularly camp on the south coast with my extended family over weeks in the summer, and one year all it did was rain, day after day, reducing our camp site to mud and water. My aunties collected shells in buckets and crushed the shells, adding spit and water until they made a rudimentary concrete that they laid underneath our tents so we could stay on longer that year.

The value of this shell resource was not lost on the colonists, who used it to build the very foundations of the colony. They were building modern Australia from countless stories, camp fires and meals shared over 65,000 years. This is building on country as a usurper, not a collaborator. The colonists came and appropriated a site and its contents for their own purposes: to re-create the buildings, farms and landscapes of their British homeland on an ancient site that had nourished the Cadigal people physically and spiritually for millennia. The purpose of the new buildings was to honour the memories of other places far away, with a different climate and different plant and animal species. The places were renamed, which meant that the knowledge and meanings encrypted in the First Nations' language of places was overlaid, often with simplistic descriptions of a site's function, as in Cattle Point; such a practice completely changed and confused the identity of the locations. Even the renaming of Tubow-gule to Bennelong Point in the early 1790s, after the senior Eora man who became an interlocutor between the natives and

British, has done little to show the true meaning of the place 'where the knowledge waters meet'.

For many years, building practices in Australia have overlaid international styles on this land, but there is now a growing movement to understand the stories and original names. In Australia, the term 'Country' has recently been capitalised in many written sources, in an attempt to carve out a different way of engaging with place. There is genuine interest in diving deep into the rich and complex culture of Indigenous people, especially their ecological relationship to the land.

In the Indigenous worldview, Country means a way of seeing the world. Everything is living. There is no separation between people and nature. It is multidimensional and extends beyond 'the ground'. There is sea, land and sky Country. As anthropologist Deborah Bird Rose wrote, 'People talk about country in the same way that they would talk about a person: they speak to country, sing to country, visit country, worry about country, feel sorry for country, and long for country.'[1] Country has Dreaming, origins and a future. The term attempts to encapsulate a sophisticated spiritual connection that Indigenous people have with the land that extends beyond ecology and includes songs, stories and kinship relationships. Paul writes more about this later in the chapter.

So what does it mean to build 'on Country'?

We realise now how the British colonists blanketed Indigenous lands with their values, placed layers of concrete, steel and glass over the earth with little understanding of its need for care, and believed in the dominance of humans over nature in their approach to architecture and planning. It can be seen in the grid layouts of townships all across Australia, the streetscapes and human-made parks, with buildings turning their backs to the rivers, and roads filling in streams. Streetscapes were favoured over landscapes. Cities like Sydney are lacquered with so many impermeable layers of Western thinking that architects, designers and builders must decide how each new layer can dig below the surface and reveal the original story of Country. How can we, as designers, pick the scabs and allow the country to breathe again?

Just as trees, mountains and rivers contain stories, the design of new places, objects and systems can be a purposeful extension of Country and imbue meaning and story into them, so that as we engage with them over time, multiple narratives are strengthened. If the stories are rooted in cultural values that reinforce our relationship to nature and compel us to care for it, then this will ultimately become our collective and cultural identity.

What a transformational perspective for Australian designers and architects: to be part of an Australian design ethos that views the construction of the built environment as an extension of our creation stories, that these 'things' are to be sung into existence with a purpose of clarity that reinforces our connection to Country and our ecological responsibility to care for it.

The framework of Indigenous culture is not just a collection of songs, stories and myths from the 'noble savage'. What we know now, through our genuine engagement and deep listening, is that beyond the dots in the paintings and the etymology of the languages is a network of symbols that reveal traditional knowledges – knowledges that have allowed Indigenous people to survive successfully despite major changes in climate, with a culture that is responsive to and coherent with nature.

And the potential goes further. The arrangement of knowledges within the environment – built *and* grown – has been achieved through Songlines as a method of recording vast amounts of ecological data without the written word. In the first book in this series, *Songlines: The Power and Promise*, co-author Lynne Kelly describes how Indigenous Australians used the three-dimensional world around them – mountains, rocks, rivers, stars – as visual triggers to remember traditional knowledge. This was further reinforced through songs, elaborate Dreaming stories and dance, so that as people moved repeatedly through Country over time, that knowledge was embedded into the synapses of their brains.

Perhaps here is the vital clue to the true meaning behind Tu-bow-gule. Maybe it was a clearing house for knowledge about marine ecology that connected to Songlines within and beyond the Sydney area, so when the *nawi* (traditional bark canoes) pulled up on the shores of what is now called Circular Quay, people gathered, shared and updated this knowledge around the camp fire.

When Jørn Utzon conceptualised the Sydney Opera House as looking like shells growing out of the ocean and as a gathering place for song and dance, you could imagine that he was connecting with the memory of Tu-bow-gule. Within his practice, he often looked to nature for guidance and cited shells, birds' wings and clouds as inspiration for his building designs. Although his homage seems purely aesthetic, Utzon was a pioneer of sustainable architecture in that he used prefabricated modular forms; his reverence for nature was not skin deep. I am sure he would have loved the chance to sit with traditional owners at Tu-bow-gule and share a meal or even spend the night and discuss how his building could be activated through ceremony and song. Imagine if the decision-makers and architects had joined them under the stars – perhaps the process of building the Opera House would have been a lot smoother.

Country-focused design is an attempt to reinvigorate ancient conversations about the human connection to nature and how the built environment can play a vital part in this dialogue. It is as much a process as it is a product, in that it goes beyond stylised homage to plants and animals. From the first marks on the page to the decisions by governments, to the materials used in the fabric of the buildings and the public domain, every step has respect for Country at its core.

It is not too late to tap into the traditional knowledge waters at Tu-bow-gule, to define a new Australian design identity – one that truly responds to the ebb and flow of Country and is powered by some very old ideas.

THE SPIRIT OF OBJECTS

It's not very often that you learn something that completely changes your whole perspective on life. This happened to me a few years ago when I interviewed Margo Neale, Senior Indigenous Curator at the National Museum of Australia, co-author of *Songlines* and the editor of the First Knowledges series. We were sitting in an amazing space at the museum that held a vast collection of artefacts, some dating from thousands of years ago. I asked Margo what I thought was a simple question about the relationship between Aboriginal people and objects. What she said transformed my thinking about the world around me and my role as a designer in it:

> In the Aboriginal worldview, everything is living. So everything is a manifestation of some other living part. And, of course, if it's objects that are made, then they're made by somebody and invested from the person who's making it and everyone who came before, like the ancestors. It's like the ancestors are actually making it. The artist or the maker is simply the medium through which this channelling takes place. If the objects go into ceremony, then they become totally vitalised, whatever stories it lives into or whatever stories it becomes part of, life after life, until it becomes, over hundreds of years, this really vital living object that has all these layers and layers of life stories inside. So what you make, why you make it, how you make it, when you make it, is all part of this ancestral cycle of life.[2]

As a creator of physical things, I felt the gravity and responsibility of my role in society shift immediately on hearing Margo's words. When you are told that your job is inseparable from your spirituality, it forces you to re-evaluate how you approach your decisions. Of course, for initiated Indigenous people this is common sense, but I had to unlearn four years of design training to get my head around the idea. The problem for me was that while I had accepted that Aboriginal spirituality was intrinsically linked to nature, I found it difficult to extend this holistic order to human-made objects.

I realised that our spirituality hinges on our relationship to the environment, which can be either built or grown.

The National Museum of Australia has exhibited a powerful film showing an old man, Frank Gurrmanamana, from Djunawunya in Arnhem Land, making a fish trap. While he makes it, he sings it into life and talks to it like it is an ancestor. He describes the sites that the ancestors made, drawing on the power of the fish-trap ancestors to make his trap. It is a ceremony, a meaningful conversation with the object that reinforces the mnemonic. As he makes it, he becomes it, so it is more than just remembering.

Margo explained how it is not just the creation of an object but its life span that is important, using as an example the story of Richard Luarkie from the Laguna tribe of New Mexico. He and his tribespeople would not accept the repatriation of objects from the Smithsonian Institution as the objects did not have enough provenance to ensure they were safe to re-enter the community. They might have been cursed and could bring harm, or injured in their journey and angry at the community who failed in their responsibility to protect the objects from being taken in the first place. This expands the notion of the conservation of artefacts as purely physical.

The human relationship to objects over their life cycle and their interconnectedness with the environment is a critical lens through which to view Aboriginal spirituality: it is not a separate metaphysical philosophy but, rather, how these relational networks are bound together. Dr Scott Mitchell, Head of Culture, Conservation and Business Services at the Australian Museum in Sydney, noted that scholars who have written about Central Australia describe:

sacred objects as the literal manifestation of the Dreamtime ancestors that created the Earth – not a representation of the ancestors, but the ancestors transformed; not just a key to ceremonial life, but also a key to life itself. There are ceremonies that cannot be performed without the proper object, in the same way they cannot be performed without the proper people.

As part of a living culture, in a sense, these objects have a life of their own. They don't belong in a museum.[3]

Conversations with our spirit ancestors often start with the collection of a material. For example, Paul describes later in this chapter how Jackson Jacob from Mornington Island, when he was harvesting wood for a boomerang, apologised to the tree.

The philosophy that objects are containers of energy is shared with other international Indigenous cultures. In his book *Blackfoot Physics*, F David Peat explains that for the Blackfoot people of the north-eastern United States:

Spirits, powers and beings can manifest themselves in a variety of different forms. Masks, rocks, knives, canoes, animals and humans can act as containers for these energies. Thus, reality, as it is experienced by The People, goes far beyond surface forms and involves a much deeper level of processes and transformation.[4]

Peat's comparative analysis of Native science and Western science finds connection in quantum and particle physics, especially in the animate nature of objects.

Peat's associate Dr Leroy Little Bear, in his 2014 talk 'Indigenous Knowledge and Western Science', explains how in Blackfoot culture:

> everything is animate. In Blackfoot there is no such thing as inanimate. Whereas in Western thought, you and I may be animate. We agree to that. Those animals out there may be animate. But are the trees? We are not too sure, some of us might say yes and some of us might say no. But the rocks, definitely, are inanimate. But in quantum physics ... in their labs, they do agree that maybe those subatomic particles do 'know' and are aware.[5]

Little Bear defines Indigenous spirituality in relation to energy waves:

> In Western physics, we talk about things in terms of matter ... whereas in Blackfoot, everything is about waves and when we really examine those energy waves, they are all about what we would refer to and translate as spirit. That is why native people are always very closely associated with the notion of spirituality.[6]

He expands to distinguish the idea that while holistic thinking and relational networks are intrinsic to Native thought, Western science is reductionist and therefore compartmentalises knowledge.

Science is about bringing the unknown into the known and then reinforcing that knowledge through observation and repetition. We know through the depth and breadth of Indigenous knowledges in Australia that First Nations people have been practising science for millennia. If technology is applied science, then the making of objects stems from the scientific knowledge. But in contrast to the science and technology of the Western world, Indigenous technology is layered with knowledge beyond the science from which it is derived. It is encoded with information that is culturally and ecologically essential. This information is ceremonially reinforced through storytelling during the making of objects, so the objects become mnemonics for the knowledge. This is why the 'factories' of Indigenous peoples, the vast scatterings of stone tools that have been archaeologically recorded on beaches and deserts all over the country, were also sites of significance – places where ceremonies were conducted and countless songs were sung as these tools for living were made. These objects became part of the family and the totemic kinship system – a network that determines people's relationship to one another and their responsibilities to the earth.

The idea that objects are animate and that they have spirit is an important concept to get your head around before we start to look at culturally appropriate approaches to traditional architecture and contemporary urban design. Those words of wisdom from Margo all those years ago sent me on an expansive journey to find the links between the tangible and the intangible and learn how the pen of a culturally 'woke' designer could somehow be a bridge between them.

THE INGENIOUS RETURNING BOOMERANG

When I ponder how Indigenous people invented things, I often think about the origins of the design of the returning boomerang, one of the world's early aerofoils. An aerofoil is 'any surface ... designed to help in lifting or controlling an aircraft or sailing boat by making use of the current of air through which it moves'.[7] Both wings of a returning boomerang have an aerofoil-shaped cross-section just like an aircraft wing. The boomerang is flat on one side but curved on the other with one edge thicker, which helps it to stay in the air due to lift. Lift is generated as the air flowing up over the curved side of the wing has further to travel than the air flowing past the flat side. The air moving over the curved surface has to travel more quickly in order to reach the other edge of the wing.

The returning boomerang is an interesting object compared to a conventional aerofoil because it spins from its centre as it flies, so the amount of lift changes across its flying surfaces. The two sides of a boomerang have different air speeds flowing over them: as it spins, the aerodynamic forces acting upon it are uneven. This causes the section of the boomerang moving in the same direction as the direction of forward motion to move faster through the air than the section moving in the opposite direction. These uneven forces make the boomerang start to turn in and follow a circular route, eventually heading back to the thrower. South Australian Museum senior curator Philip Jones writes, 'The returning boomerang shares its aeronautical principles with a flying discus, a banking airplane, a propeller, a helicopter and a gyroscope. Few mechanical inventions display so many scientific laws.'[8]

How was this sophisticated piece of engineering designed? Was it one person's light-bulb moment? Did it come from the observation of birds flying, studying the structure of their wings, or from watching how leaves fall from trees? Was it dreamt in an altered state of consciousness during ceremony? It required someone to find the right kind of wood, shape the wood incrementally, throw it, shape it a bit more, throw it again and refine it, for who knows how long. Either way, the idea was born from Indigenous peoples' deep connection to Country.

The process of trial and error led to something that can be considered one of the most amazing flying machines of all time. The same design principles are seen in the wings of the massive aircraft that get around our skies today. This was the work of early aeronautical engineers, improving performance incrementally over countless iterations, marking the beginning of a technological society.

BOOMERANGS IN STORY AND SONG

PAUL MEMMOTT

I first started learning about boomerangs – what they are, how they come from Country and how they relate to particular people – in the early 1970s. On Mornington Island in the Wellesley Islands of Queensland, the homeland and home seas of the Lardil people, I was befriended by a relatively young but eminent law man, Jackson Jacob. His Lardil name was Thungalgunyaldin, meaning the leaf debris and *guna* (faeces) left under trees by flying foxes (literally 'flying fox droppings'). Jackson's Aboriginal skin classification was Palyarinyi, and I was to learn later that he was in a brother-in-law relationship to me (my skin is Kamarangi).[9] He became a keen consultant for my PhD research but our contact was cut short a few years later when he died prematurely from kidney disease in his thirties.

At that time, I had struck up a relationship with the head photographer/cinematographer of the Australian Museum, Howard Hughes, who was interested in coming to Mornington Mission to make some short ethnographic films. Jackson and Howard were excited about working together and I was conscripted to assist in a creative capacity. One of the films was titled *The Boomerang*. In it, Jackson demonstrated the meticulous process of instilling the aerodynamic form into a comeback, or returning, boomerang by charring the shaped artefact in a fire to burn off excess layers of wood and then scraping back the char. He used a knife for this but traditionally the Lardil and other people of the neighbouring Tangkic language groups used a piece of baler shell with a serrated edge, shaped by breaking off pieces of shell between their teeth (they protected their teeth with a piece of paperbark). He spent considerable time heating the near-completed boomerang in the fire and then twisting its two 'legs' in opposite directions to perfect its aerodynamic design to his satisfaction. Jackson taught me to throw a returning boomerang using a specific arm action and angle of grip and launching it at about 45 degrees into the direction of the prevailing wind.

At one point in the filming, when Jackson was demonstrating how to cut a raw piece of wood from the lower trunk of a *kurrburu* tree (*Acacia alleniana*; see Figure 1), he made a revelatory statement: 'When I do this I have to sing to the tree, to the old spirit in the tree,

FIGURE 1: Jackson Jacob (since deceased) extracts part of the trunk and root of a *kurrburu* tree, using an axe and a tomahawk as a wedge, 1975.

to say I'm sorry for cutting out a piece of him; but then his spirit will remain inside the boomerang.' After Jackson died, a number of elders furnished explanations for this, not the least of whom was my adoptive father, Lindsay Roughsey, aka Burrud (meaning 'seaweed'). But it was not till the early 1980s, when I was developing a culture teaching package and book for secondary schools, that I was given the most complete explanation, by my Kamarangi skin brother Henry Peters (Wunhun, or beach oak), who authorised its use in teaching throughout Australia.

The kurrburu tree had grown from the ribs of Thuwathu, the Rainbow Serpent, in the Dreaming. Thuwathu was originally human, according to Lardil law, and came to Gununa (Mornington Island) from the mainland with members of his family at the end of the dry season. They made a camp of windbreaks on the south side of the island in hot dusty weather. However, rather than build a *wungkurr* (windbreak), Thuwathu chose to build a *ngampirr* (an enclosed wet-weather shelter), much to the amusement of his family. Nevertheless and sure enough, within a few days a big storm built, fast and unexpectedly. Thuwathu retreated into his ngampirr while the others were caught short, with insufficient firewood to burn in the torrential rain. In particular, his sister Bulthuku (Willy Wagtail) became distressed because her newborn baby began shivering and sneezing and eventually developed a 'hotness' (high temperature). She went to the door of Thuwathu's ngampirr three or four times and pleaded with him to let her place her baby in a visible piece of unoccupied space, but each time he said, 'No, sister, go away. That space is for my knee' (or arm or head or foot, whatever the case, on her successive attempts). Eventually the baby died, and in her state of extreme grief and anger, Bulthuku lit Thuwathu's ngampirr with a firestick and he was burnt alive inside, with the structure collapsing on him. Thuwathu emerged in a charcoaled state, in agony, and crawled through the country, carving out a riverbed (now called Dugong

River). As he travelled, his rib bones broke out and embedded in the ground, transforming into kurrburu trees. He metamorphosed into the Rainbow Serpent, emerging and remaining to this day in the sea surrounding the Wellesley Islands archipelago.

There is much more to this sacred history, not least of which is a moral analysis of both the brother's and sister's behaviour and the implications for Aboriginal law for successive generations.[10]

———

Boomerangs have a multitude of design properties that I have been fortunate enough to learn about.[11] As my adoptive Buralangi-skin father Burrud was the lead Larumbenda (windward) songman of the Lardil, I was conscripted to assist him in his role on the dance ground. This took many forms and tasks, but one is pertinent here: the use of a pair of boomerangs as a percussion instrument. When a songman with a strong voice is in full flight leading a performance of an important dance, he claps his boomerangs together forcefully in changing times and rhythms to create maximum effect. If the boomerangs are not well manufactured from the best quality hardwood (such as kurrburu wood), they will soon crack, deteriorate and break apart. Burrud thus preferred to use larger, heavier fighting boomerangs (*juluwarr*) for quality of sound rather than the thinner, lightweight comeback boomerangs (*thaankur wangal*) (see Figure 2). Being a ceremonial leader and steeped in Aboriginal cosmology, he was excited by boomerangs made by master craftspeople from places of high esteem in Aboriginal law. When I announced that I was

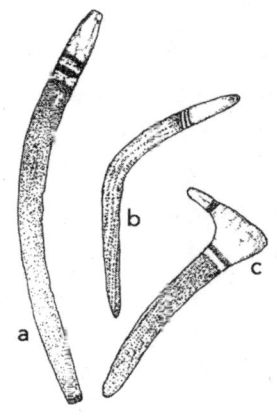

FIGURE 2: Three categories of Lardil boomerangs from Mornington Island: (a) the fighting/hunting boomerang, *julwarr*, (b) the comeback boomerang, *thacnkur wangal*, for sky hunting; and (c) the imported hooked boomerang, *mungkuburr*, for fighting.

taking a two-week break from living at Gununa in August 1975 to go to Central Australia to carry out a consultancy, he furnished me with decorated baler shells, stingray pin circumcision knives and a cassette of songs to trade for a pair of Warlpiri boomerangs and bunches of emu feathers. (Although there was an Emu sacred site on Mornington Island, created in the Dreaming, there were no living emus, hence their attractive feathers were a sought-after commodity for dance decoration.)

On reaching my destination, Yuendumu in the central-west Northern Territory, and meeting elders and translating my adoptive skin into their skin system, I was adopted by a senior man, Larry Nelson of the Jakamarra skin group. He was the team leader of the community housing work gang, and as my consultancy was on new housing, our relationship seemed a logical fit. Not only did I acquire a pair of boomerangs for Burrud, I was also presented with a pair for my own personal use, and Larry had the family clan country Dreaming painted on them. The father–son skin couple of which I became part was Jakamarra-Jupurula, and on subsequent visits in the 1970s I was taught a range of design motifs for the Dreamings of this skin pair, including Woma or carpet snake, and Nappa or rain. I have fond memories of sitting under shade shelters with renowned Warlpiri elders like Darby Jampijinpa, Denny Japaljarri and Jimija Jungarayi (all long since passed away), painting sacred designs on boomerangs and on timber shields while they sang the relevant Dreaming songs in preparation for ceremony. After ceremony the designs were often wiped off, the lesson being that the boomerangs and shields were potent objects when charged with the songs and designs, and their potency had to be neutralised for everyday handling and use.

Another important aspect of boomerang design is the nature of right- and left-handed boomerangs. A common design of a fighting boomerang is for one side to be flat and the other side gently curved. If a slab of cut timber with the appropriate elbow bend is split down the middle, it cleaves apart with two flattish surfaces, and then the outer side of both halves can be shaped into the curved boomerang profile. One side is more comfortably thrown by a right-handed thrower and the other by a left-handed thrower. Interestingly, there are sacred histories from the Dreaming in which left-handed throwers are identified as having superior powers. One such sacred history I was taught by Alyawarr elders in Central Australia pertains to a flying fox, Pitungu, who travelled in a huge circuit around the central-east Northern Territory singing hundreds of songs but then was distracted at Alpurrurulam Lake on the Georgina River (Lake Nash), where he stole two young women from the local Rat Dreaming clan (Nyumala), projecting the women forward by wrapping their hair in his woomera and hurling them a long distance, as if by a spear. He was pursued unsuccessfully for 800 kilometres by local clansmen throwing their boomerangs at him before he was eventually struck down by a left-handed boomerang thrower! Celebration followed of the skills and potency of left-handed throwers and their specially designed boomerangs. Pitungu is today the symbol of the Alpurrurulam community and used as its official logo, an important design motif from the Dreaming that is laden with meaning if one knows the hundreds of associated songs that make up Pitungu's travel epic.

Where did this potency – or what Alison has referred to earlier in this chapter as energy or spirit – come from? What is or was the Dreaming? And why and exactly how is it relevant to Aboriginal design knowledge? What do we need to know about the Dreaming to 'build on Country' in a respectful and informed way?

THE ENERGIES OF ANCESTRAL BEINGS

Australian First Nations see people and their place in the universe in a unique way. This belief system or philosophy, often called the Dreaming, is part of social, religious, political and economic life for traditional Aboriginal people. Any system of beliefs about life and the universe tries to explain difficult abstract ideas such as time, change and stability, matter and spirit, the seen and the unseen, appearance and reality, and human identity. The Dreaming philosophy defines these ideas, gives them significance and shows how they apply in daily life for Aboriginal people. Despite the variations in cultures among Aboriginal groups, many share a common belief in the Dreaming, which also explains the set of values and customs that govern correct thought and behaviour in aspects of everyday life.

To understand the Dreaming more clearly, we need to look at how it relates to both the past and the present. A first understanding is that the Dreaming refers to the ancestral past, at least some 70,000 years ago and most probably much longer, when Aboriginal people and plants and animals were adapting and evolving in a continent of changing environmental conditions. The Country is said to have been 'soft' in the Dreaming – able to be shaped. Aboriginal history is concerned with this time and contains accounts of the doings of Ancestral Beings, some of whom seem to have been animal, some human, but in most cases a combination of both: according to most Aboriginal cultures, all animals had human qualities at that time. Individuals were made up of a human and an animal or plant species, or some other natural phenomenon: a dog man, barracuda man, yam woman, tree man, moon man and so on. The Ancestral Beings (sometimes called Dreaming Heroes) were said to 'jump up' from the ground or sea. Many of them travelled about the country, interacting with each other and with the environment, experiencing adventures, making places, leaving signs of their presence – even parts of their bodies – and eventually dying and/or going into the ground, sea or sky. These activities of the ancestors are said to have left traces of their energies in the environment.

Generally speaking, every part of Country in Aboriginal Australia contains a set of travel paths crisscrossing the landscape, in which sacred places occur that were created by the ancestors. They had power to change the landscape and even to change themselves into aspects of the landscape, such as rocks and trees, which then became and remained storehouses of sacred energies, also called 'spirits' or 'life-cells' or Dreaming 'essence', associated with the particular ancestor.[12] The ancestors seemed to have unlimited sources of these energies, which were reproduced and deposited at places they made or even just touched. Energies were also left in the environment in parts of themselves, such as their blood, faeces, sperm or broken bones. The Heroes returned to the ground upon their deaths and the entire continent was covered in a network of interconnected sites. Those who view the Australian deserts or forests as 'wilderness' are thus misled, according to this philosophy.

Three types of travel patterns can be distinguished here: first, those who travelled through the environment along a particular route;[13] second, those who rose up at a place and, although travelling out regularly into the surrounding environment, always returned to it; and third, those Dreaming Heroes who rose up at a place and remained at that place.

At some point during the early Dreaming period, the dual nature of the Ancestral Beings separated. Then, for example, the kangaroo men became kangaroos and men – although men retained something of their kangaroo nature, and kangaroos kept something of their human nature. This introduces a more complex definition of the Dreaming – that is, the Dreaming is not only concerned with the time of creation, or with history: it continues into the present and into the future. It is believed that the ancestors' spirit energies remain in the landscape and in Aboriginal people. Their energy (or essence) has been passed down to today's generations. The sites and their energies are all still there, whether people know it or not – even in the large cities of Australia.

This forms the basis of the Aboriginal belief that people are bound to nature with a common life force, not separate from it; that they are part of nature, and nature is part of them. So today we can still find Aboriginal people who have a close bond with, say, a species of tree, or the kangaroo, or the barramundi. They feel they have inside themselves some of the spirit energies of the Ancestral Being. This also introduces the Aboriginal belief in descent (tracing one's ancestors downwards) from the Dreaming (both past and present). Another aspect is that for many groups, when a human dies, part of his or her spirit returns into the landscape and may once again manifest itself as a spiritual being, animal, bird or plant. Understandably, there is a belief in 'unseen people'.

The Heroes created ground paintings with specific graphic symbols for particular sites. These also contain the 'power' or sacred essence and each is characteristically associated with a particular Dreaming or Hero and the sites he or she created. The Heroes painted the same designs or symbols on shields and on their chests for performing ceremonies. They also created songs telling of their travels and adventures. The verses of many of these songs are site-specific in their references, and are or were sung as part of the ceremonies. When there is a long travel route containing many sites of a Dreaming Hero, there will be a lengthy sequence of songs to be sung: hence the term 'Songlines'.

The ceremonies have been passed down over time. Some are generally of the type that anthropologists call 'increase rituals', aimed at causing the reproduction of the particular animal, plant or other phenomenon associated with the local site and with the Hero. The term 'local totem centre' has been used by anthropologists to describe such sites. So a ceremony created by Rain Ancestors in the Dreaming would be designed to be used at Rain Dreaming sites to cause the falling of rain. Similarly, the yellow-goanna-men Heroes left behind ceremonies to make goanna procreate, to be performed at yellow goanna sites. Traditionally, there were large gatherings of people at a favoured camp that was abundant with resources, for the performance of large numbers of ceremonies, including those on very long travel lines. A characteristic feature of this category of ceremonies and their associated paraphernalia is that they are all site-specific in their identity and reference to a particular totem or Dreaming.

The Dreaming Heroes also provided the rules of social interaction and of descent, kinship, ritual property and social property (sharing resources) necessary for the maintenance of order among people. The various behavioural rules and conventions for social interaction and ritual together form what is called in Aboriginal English 'the Law'. Many of the rules are encoded in songs and sacred histories concerning the activities of the Dreaming Heroes. Ethnomusicologist Richard Moyle quotes a northern Alyawarr elder, Slippery Morton, in this regard:

If there was no Dreaming for this land, this Aboriginal land, we couldn't call out, 'Hey, mother', 'Hey, brother'. It would be dark, we would live just like dogs, with no social order. That Dreamtime gave us absolutely everything.[14]

I have been privileged to receive in-depth knowledge from the elders of particular nations about the Dreaming, and have found there to be much local complexity in all aspects from history to contemporary practice, although the general nature of the Dreaming seems to have been widely shared across the continent. The significance for design and building on Country is clear. In any part of Australia, there will be sacred places imbued with perpetual energies and associated with Ancestral Beings of particular totemic spirits. Their energies or essence can be embedded not only in and on the land or sea or sky but in materials or resources taken from that environment. Such materials can be shaped into artefacts, structures and other designed things (for example, medicines or paintings), which in turn contain and perpetuate those energies. And the same energies implanted at particular places may extend out in different directions along the Songlines crisscrossing the continent.

3

ON CAMPS, SHELTER AND COUNTRY

PAUL MEMMOTT

The traditional – or what I also call classical – Aboriginal architecture built before colonists arrived is an expression of a complex set of relationships between the physical and social environments. When the British arrived in the late 1700s, there was a set of distinct cultural regions in Aboriginal Australia corresponding with natural land systems and geographic features. In each was a body of architectural knowledge employed in settlement life. Each such regional group of knowledge can be termed 'traditional architecture' or 'ethno-architecture'. The classical Aboriginal 'architecture' was one that had been created and built by the users, adjusted as required to suit their own lifestyle and changing needs, and supportive of their own social organisation and interaction. It was all done by the people with their own technologies, labour and skills, drawing where appropriate on their customary traditions.[1]

ABORIGINAL MOVEMENT PATTERNS

Pre-colonisation, Aboriginal people moved around their own defined 'land estates' (or, on the coast, 'sea estates') or Country on a seasonal basis to exploit available foods and resources. The range of travel by Aboriginal groups was in all areas restricted by various territorial rules and by the need to maintain local religious obligations in their own Country and in the Countries of their grandparents and spouse(s). For most of the seasonal year, small local groups were scattered throughout their respective Countries engaged in hunting, gathering and (except in very arid areas) fishing. People were very conscious of and comfortable with their place within their own local territory, familiar with its geography, and spiritually attached to its sacred sites and sacred histories.

The small local Aboriginal groups formed camps that they would occupy for a single day or up to several seasons. But throughout each region of Aboriginal Australia, large-scale gatherings composed of people from several tribal or language groups – now called 'nations' by some – occasionally occurred at the larger, more reliable water sources in good seasons when sufficient food could sustain upwards of 100 people over periods of weeks. At these gatherings there occurred feasting, trading, celebrations, ceremonies, initiations, arrangement of marriages, settlement of disputes, and forms of emotional reconciliation. The behavioural rules were at their most complex in such large camps. In these settings, people sought and experienced social kindness and friendship through the development and maintenance of relationships involving both voluntary and obligatory exchanges.

The mobile hunter-gatherer lifestyle often resulted in relatively impermanent architecture, but for those in localities with plentiful food resources, there was a tendency to establish more permanent camps,[2] which were often seasonally occupied. Inclement weather resulted in more elaborate architecture in such semi-sedentary camps.

Another consequence of the mobile hunter-gatherer lifestyle was the need for lightweight, versatile toolkits. The design of the overall set of artefacts in the toolkit and how they worked together was just as important as the design of individual artefacts. More on this in Chapter 5.

CLASSICAL ABORIGINAL ARCHITECTURE

The dominant architectural types in Aboriginal settlements prior to the British invasion were domestic, comprising a range of shelter types and other structures used in residential camps. The occupation of camp sites from a single day to several months with largely impermanent architecture was often misread by early colonists as a confirmation of lack of connection or attachment to place. However, each small local Aboriginal group occupied a defined series of camps in an ongoing pattern of regular seasonal rotation.

Most language groups employed a repertoire of up to seven or eight shelter types and sometimes more (for example, in the Top End: see Figure 3). Shelters were selected for construction and use under particular circumstances of prevailing weather, availability of local raw materials, planned purpose and length of stay, and size and composition of the group to be accommodated. Each shelter type had a regional distribution, particular styles being largely a function of the available structural and cladding materials (tree limbs, barks, grasses, foliage, vines, stones, soils) and the extent of dominant climatic influences. The customary settlement patterns of shelter design, technology, seasonal usage and camp behaviour were familiar and repetitive, and constituted part of the cultural template of everyday life.

FIGURE 3: Examples of Yolŋu Aboriginal shelters and dwellings, including vaulted roof types, in Arnhem Land, northern Australia.[3]

Camp size varied from a single family up to several hundred people. In a typical larger-sized settlement, separate shelters were commonly used for day and night activities. During the day, men and women congregated apart; nuclear families resided together at night. Unmarried men and women slept separately in their respective gendered groups. At night, the domestic groups were spatially segmented into clusters for sleeping as either nuclear families, single men or single women (see Figure 4). Further levels of clustering in larger camps were based on class identity, tribal identity or close kinship relationships (see Chapter 6). Nevertheless, the groups were usually close enough for visual and aural communication. At the same time, there were kinship rules that forbade specific relatives from camping in proximity to one another, generating unique

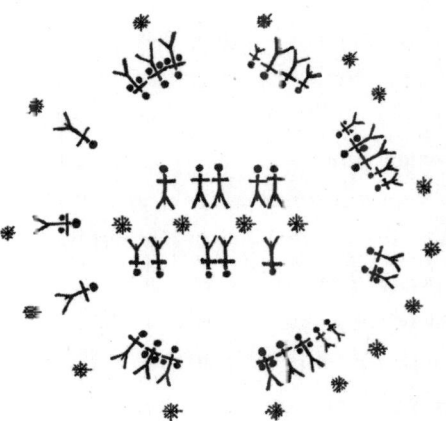

FIGURE 4: Lardil mosquito camp layout for a large camping party or a 'long camp', sited in a setting open to breezes. Single men are clustered together in the middle. Smoke from the many fires repels the mosquitoes.

types of social-spatial behaviour. Movement around camps was also restricted by rules or protocols about where particular people could go, for example gender-exclusive ceremonial grounds. The 'sociospatial' patterns of Aboriginal settlements can thus be defined as the customary division into spatial zones, each area occupied by a number of household groups and possessing some common social identity and a characteristic social structure. Figure 19 in Chapter 6 shows an example of the layout of a large camp in Arrernte Country.

When people departed and travelled on to fresh camp sites, the shelters were usually left standing – at least their frames, if not their cladding. A widespread practice in forested country was to remove rigid sheets of bark from shelters after use, lay them flat and weight them with logs to prevent them from warping or blowing away.[4] A shelter could then be rebuilt within minutes upon a return visit to a camp site. This was further facilitated by the use of a durable timber species for the frame, which often remained standing for many years: examples of such frames are still being encountered in the Simpson Desert region, where some have stood for the best part of a century. Objects that were not required at the next camp or that were too cumbersome to carry were left behind – for example, grinding stones and nets. Such personal possessions were not touched by others.[5]

A survey of the various cultural regions reveals such technologies as stone wall construction, grass thatching and plaiting, split bamboo, woven pandanus and coconut-palm leaf, clay and mud plastering, excavated floors, earth platforms, sand-weighted roofs, split-cane ties and the weaving of foliage between wall rails. The diversity of construction techniques defies the ethnocentric notion that Aboriginal people did not make a conscious effort to utilise their local environment. Environmental management was mediated by religious links to sites and areas, imbuing particular groups with responsibilities to monitor and ensure natural resources were not depleted, and to facilitate (often ritually) a regeneration of supply stocks.

DOMESTIC ARCHITECTURAL TYPES

In pleasant weather, a recurring preference across Australia was for open living with minimal structures. A widespread design for cold, windy weather was the grass or foliage windbreak with warming fires (see Figure 5). Shade structures were also widely used, and constructed by implanting leafy boughs in the ground or erecting a horizontal roof structure or making a lean-to with a ridgepole.

FIGURE 5: A windbreak with a wall extension added after a change of wind direction: 'a' is the original wind direction, and 'b' is the new wind direction.

A domed shade was built throughout the Western Desert by securing the stems of bushy limbs in a roughly circular floor plan, curving inwards to form a thick roof. This shelter not only provided shade but allowed outward vision and airflow while filtering out flies.

Low enclosed shelters provided protection in those parts of the continent where rain only fell for several days or weeks. Shelter heights were consistently 1.2 to 1.5 metres, for lying or sitting postures. Wider-span structures were also low and used for large domestic groups (single men, single women, multiple family groups). Structural forms reflected the type of materials available for their construction and included domes, rectilinear or cubic huts, and cones with or without central support posts. Unsupported forms of stiff bark included the barrel vault made of curved sheets (half-cylinder form) and the gable made of folded sheets (triangular prism form). Domes were up to 3.6 metres in diameter to suit the size of the occupant group. Frameworks of heavy rigid curved boughs were commonly employed in the arid interior. On the east coast, frames of saplings were lightweight for both dome and cone forms. Claddings used in eastern and northern coastal areas comprised a range of barks, tussock grasses, reeds and palm leaves. Common cladding materials of the interior were hummock and tussock grasses, sometimes with a coating of sand, mud or clay. Triangular prism forms were built in open forests of the Arnhem Land hinterland with ridgepoles fixed between tree trunks carrying rafters, clad with foliage and all sealed with a layer of smoothed white clay.[6]

However, in certain places across the continent there were technologically crafted styles of strong weatherproof shelters, sufficiently high to stand in, and supporting sedentary or semi-sedentary occupation. In some cases these structures covered large floor areas to permit occupation by several families or a gendered group, facilitating internal social interaction during the day. The reasons for the development of such styles varied but seem related to the occurrence of long periods of inclement weather with continual rain (even snow), which may have also reduced mobility; the presence of an abundance of resources[7] to enable long-term local residence; and the social motivation to sustain large-scale gatherings for ceremony and other purposes. Ethnographers also saw tribal or clan base camps whose populations fluctuated but that were continually occupied by at least some people all year round, even if only a few.

In the largest and wettest tract of old tropical rainforest on the continent – for example, in north-eastern Australia – clusters of interconnected domes were made of lattice cane or sapling frames and clad with layers of thatched grass or palm leaves or bark (see Figure 6). Similarly, on the inclement south-west Tasmanian coast, winter domes were grass-thatched, lined internally with paperbark and up to 3.6 metres in diameter and 2.4 metres high, with a small entrance opening. Some western Victorian domes were of a similar size, earth-clad, cupola-shaped, often fitted with a porch, and with a circular smoke vent at the apex, covered with a sod. (A comparable type was seen in parts of the south-western coast of the continent.) Also in western Victoria, low circular stone walls were constructed to carry timber-framed roofs (see Figure 7). These taller structures had to be of sufficient strength to bear the weight of an adult carrying out roof maintenance after bad weather. There are further locations

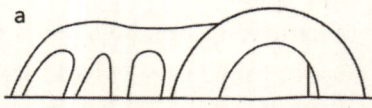

a

Intersecting dome type with multiple entrances

b

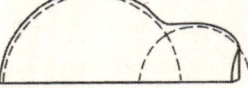

Elevation

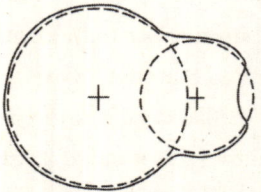

Plan – attached entrance dome type

FIGURE 6: Camp in woodland not far from a mountainous rainforest area at Bellenden Ker in Yidindji Country (near Gordonvale, Queensland), c.1904. The structures involve complex forms of intersecting domes. For example, the structure at the centre rear has a large internal space with at least four doorways, possibly for use by different co-wives in a polygynous marriage – see sketch (a). The shelter on the left has an entrance porch made of a small dome attached to the main dome – see sketch (b).

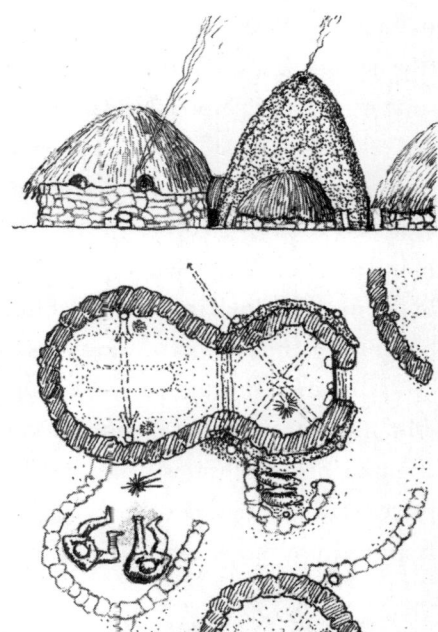

FIGURE 7: A hypothetical reconstruction of a Gunditjmara house in western Victoria, with stone wall and timber-framed, domed roof clad in peat sods.

where the presence of concentrated resources appears to have been more of a determinant than the inclement weather. An example is the 15-metre-diameter, 1.8-metre-high dome observed in 1824 at a beach camp on North Stradbroke Island, Queensland, adjacent to a seasonal mullet-school netting channel.[8]

Several wet-weather examples from the northern monsoonal coasts exemplify the influence of materials on form. The two most suitable claddings were paperbark (*Melaleuca*) and stringybark (*Eucalyptus*). Paperbark was flexible in two directions and therefore suitable for domes (which would be filled with smoke to keep out mosquitoes). Stringybark sheets could only be bent in one direction (the best species for this was *E. tetrodonta*), resulting in vaulted roofs supported on single, double or triple ridgepoles. A sleeping platform was often constructed under such a vault to avoid boggy ground, and fires were burnt underneath to repel mosquitoes. Shelters were also used for protecting respectively the bodies or skeletons of the dead, hunting dogs and supplies of grain. Tree-platform camps were used in flood-prone areas in the Gulf of Carpentaria and in the Arafura Swamp in Arnhem Land during goose-egg harvesting.

It is now unusual to see examples of classical Aboriginal ethno-architecture that do not incorporate Western materials and components, exceptions being windbreaks and shades in remote places, and Aboriginal cultural centres, where the old shelters are displayed as forms of cultural tourism.

SHELTER AND SETTLEMENT PATTERNS IN TRADITIONAL ABORIGINAL SOCIETIES

In much of Aboriginal Australia, traditional shelters were used as tools to shield the activities of everyday life from inclement weather (rain, snow, hot and cold winds, hot sun). As such, they were pleasurable and secure things for the time they were used. Their life span seldom exceeded a season and, on most of the continent, was more often several weeks or less. Although timber-frame structures may have endured through several seasons, they would ultimately collapse under white-ant attack, or be used as firewood or as components in a new shelter.

It seems that for many Aboriginal groups – unlike many other cultures – symbolism was seldom attached to shelters, nor were they often embellished with any decoration (although important exceptions to this are discussed in Chapter 4). For most groups, shelters were not a 'home' in the Western sense of being a permanent structure for protection against climate and other physical hazards, and to which are attached personal decorations, colours, symbols and social status. For most Aboriginal people, a sense of home and security, and domestic memories and experiences, were more regularly associated with specific camp sites, their position in the cultural landscape (or Country), and the routines of domestic behaviour and techniques of shelter design – not with any specific shelters, which were too many, too similar and too impermanent to provide such a wealth of stable links with the past. Indeed, each family or individual had access to a repertoire of camp sites in their own Country, to any of which they could withdraw if they required social retreat or solitude (for example, after a conflict or to focus on intra-family kindness). Conversely, they could join up at the more popular and resource-rich base camps used in particular seasons to host large social gatherings that included visitors from surrounding tribal groups.

In the most inclement parts of the continent, characterised by lengthy periods of rain (often cold rain, and sometimes snow), more permanent forms of shelters were employed in semi-sedentary camps (see Figure 8) and were likely to have been personalised and decorated. Examples of such regions are western Tasmania, south-western Victoria, south-west Western Australia and the north

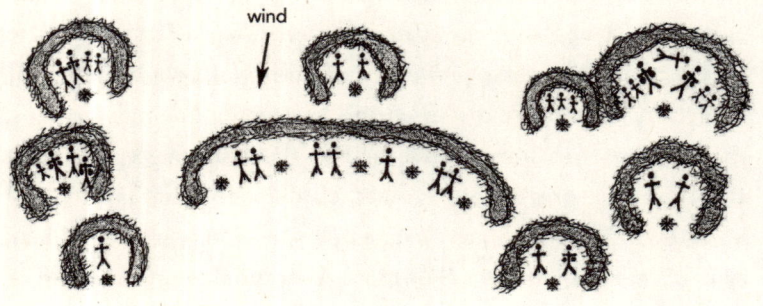

FIGURE 8: Cold-weather camp showing sleeping arrangements in windbreaks (with 13 hearths).

Queensland rainforest. The internal painting of the bark walls of wet-season shelters has been seen in Arnhem Land and western and central Tasmania, as has the use of internal feathering in the latter region.

THE KINDNESS OF CAMP SITES

The life of the Aboriginal architect-builder represents a cultural triumph of sustainable design practice. Camps provided settings with sufficient autonomy to maintain and practise Aboriginality into the colonial era. Every so often, due to residential mobility, population changes, births and deaths, climatic shifts, natural calamities, or settlement 'fission' resulting from intergroup conflicts, the need arose to regenerate the settlement, recycle the old building materials and rebuild the shelters. The people not only designed and built their own residences but also planned their locations and spacing in relation to one another in a settlement.

This settlement lifestyle results in a more essential, direct and demanding relationship with the environment than does that of the average Western urban dweller, who has little control over the shaping of their environment, and who prefers a secured and sealed retreat when the elements rage. The settlement lifestyle reveals more clearly something of the essential nature of Aboriginal humanness and experience, which requires a more intense personal confrontation and involvement with each and every problem of residential survival that is experienced due to day-to-day natural weather cycles and climatic events. It is a lifestyle that is secured within the perceived kindness and familiarity of a repertoire of home camp sites and cultural landscapes created and energised by Dreaming Heroes.

4

ENGINEERED STRUCTURES

PAUL MEMMOTT

A vast array of engineered structures were designed and employed by Aboriginal societies in pre-colonisation times. They included ground hunting hides, bird catching hides,[1] rock-wall fisheries, ground ovens, wells, storage platforms and posts, ceremonial stone arrangements, circular mounds, stone quarries, ochre pits and middens, as well as foliage walls, nets, trenches and pitfalls for trapping game. Structures of the Barkandji (also Barkindji or Paakantyi) people of the Barka or Darling River, for example, included wickerwork and rock-wall dams for catching fish, walls of foliage to direct the movement of terrestrial animals into nets and pitfalls, and very large nets erected across streams to catch flocks of birds, while small shelters were sometimes built of timber and bark sheeting over water soakages in the dry season to prevent evaporation.[2]

VALUES IN ROCK

From my high tent camp on Dijingiya hill in the Wellesley Islands, where I was given the Lardil name of Birdibil (Bone Moon) in 1973, I used to often see old Kaiadilt women walking along the beach to a curved line of rocks exposed at low tide on the muddy sea bottom. They foraged for crabs along the boulder wall, which was caked in oysters, and occasionally built the wall up in places with more rocks. One day I went down to watch. We greeted each other as best we could, but the women did not speak English and I did not speak Kaiadilt. In a gesture of goodwill, I assisted in building the long wall up in a few places. They clearly approved, grinning and chatting away incessantly. I came back to do this on other days wearing my sandals after experiencing infected foot cuts from oyster shells. This was the unwitting start of my study of Tangkic fish traps.

The Wellesley fish traps were first recorded in the 1890s by new settlers, who described them as a 'succession of walled-in paddocks of many acres in extent'.[3] How do these traps work? They take many shapes, but the norm is a roughly semicircular rock wall built to a height of up to 1 metre, cemented in place by oysters with the trap ends pointing towards the land side (the fish trap on the map in Figure 24 in Chapter 7 is an example of this). When the tide comes in, the water covers well over the trap and fish come shoreward; then, as the tide recedes and the water drops below the wall, fish are caught inside the trap and easily collected with a spear or nets.

It sounds simple, but it is more complex than it seems. A wide range of tidal conditions exist in the southern Gulf of Carpentaria. Most days there is only one tide, but for 1–3 days in every 11 or 12 days, there are two. During these double tides relatively little water movement occurs, but at 'springs' (twice in a lunar month) the tidal range reaches 2.6 to 3.7 metres.[4] These patterns are even more irregular in the wet season due to the frequent outflowing of huge quantities of fresh water from rivers into the Gulf, as well as the impact of tidal surges generated from cyclones.

Every Kaiadilt clan group utilised rock-wall traps (*ngurruwarra*), but those who specialised most in rock-wall fish-trap design overcame the tidal problem by building two or three traps extending from the land so that at least one trap could be relied upon whatever the tidal regime. They also speared turtle and dugong (sea cows) inside the traps with specially designed barbed spearheads. The Lardil, on the other hand, appear to have had only a single-wall trap solution: if the tides didn't suit, they relied on other technologies – such as large nets and spearing – to catch fish. They also used one or more large nets rather than rock-wall traps to catch dugong, and did not have specialised dugong spears. The Lardil were thus less dependent on the traps and appear to have relied more on group hunting strategies; they had far fewer traps than the Kaiadilt. There were clearly two different technological design strategies employed by neighbouring groups evolving over time. The Kaiadilt believed the original trap design in their sea Country was instigated by Bujuku (black crane) and Kaarku (seagull) in the Dreaming.

Rock-wall fish traps were also built on freshwater rivers and in other coastal locations in Australia. Figure 9 shows *ngunnhu* or fish traps in the Barwon River at Brewarrina, close to the tribal territories of the Wangaaypuyan, Wailwan, Kamilaroi/Gamilaraay and Muruwari. Their sacred history tells how the Supreme Ancestral Being cast his fishing net over the river and thereby instructed his two sons how to design the traps. He named each rock-wall trapping pen and allocated it to a particular clan or family who was responsible for its maintenance. The design allows for operation in both high and low river flows, the former being very fast. The solid-black forms in Figure 9 are large, named in-situ rocks. It was believed that in the vicinity of the Kirragurra rock there resided spirit beings capable of causing sickness or misfortune, and that they guarded the fisheries

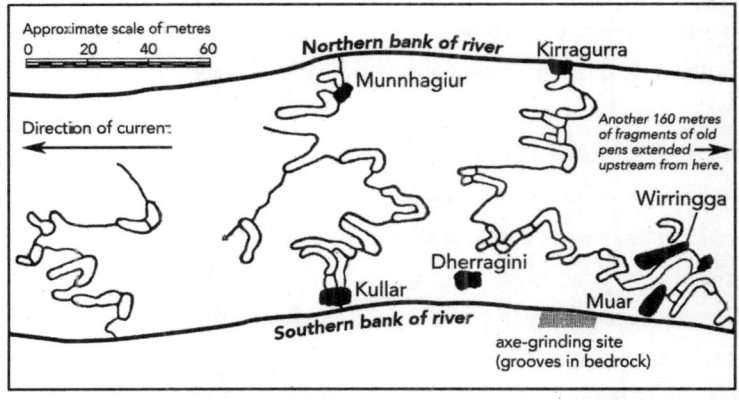

FIGURE 9: Rock-wall fish traps in freshwater Country on the Barwon River, New South Wales.

against strangers. The ngunnhu are a significant example of how cultural and social meanings are encoded in Aboriginal engineering.

But how did these traps work? Hunters were on the alert as to when schools of fish were seasonally travelling upstream to spawn. When large schools were passing, 'gates' in the walls were closed by blocking them with large rocks. Once fish were in the larger pools, the hunters would hit the water to scare the fish into hiding in the small pens (which were 5 to 20 metres in length) where they could be easily speared. The traps in the middle of the river were relatively low so as to be usable in a slow-flowing river run, while the traps closer to the banks were higher for use in a flooded river run.

VALUES IN FIBRE

Since 2007, I have been running cultural workshops for young First Nations adults at the Dugalunji Camp near Camooweal. The camp is operated by the Myuma group of corporations, owned by the Indjalandji-Dhidhanu people of the upper Georgina Basin. Each year, some three or four pre-vocational training programs are held, with jobs in the construction or mining industries awaiting the trainees. I attend for several days during the twelve- or fourteen-week program to conduct workshops with a team of Aboriginal mentors and an elder. We always carry out a good share of the learning experiences on Country, and always visit the sacred lakes of the Georgina. These lakes are large perennial waterholes, usually teeming with birdlife. In pre-European-contact times (and for some decades after), they were Indjalandji heartland base camps that at the peak of the annual seasonal cycle could support big trading and ceremonial gatherings attended by neighbouring groups such as the Bularnu, Wakaya, Alyawarr, Waluwara, Waanyi and Kalkatungu. When standing next to the waterlily-covered home of Thuwani, the Rainbow Serpent, the surrounding country alive with animals, I ask the trainees how they think the Old People caught food here. After a lot of guessing on their part, I start to share knowledge on the advanced netting practices and the cunning use of constructed foliage races in the vicinity of the lakes.

I worked as the anthropologist for the successful Indjalandji native title claim and various other land rights claims for neighbouring groups from the 1980s through to the early 2000s. During that time, I made an intensive study – mentored by Aboriginal elders as my teachers – of the many aspects of the culture of the region, including the technologies used in hunting, and learnt that Aboriginal people were dependent on their fibre expertise and knew how to manufacture all sizes and design types of nets and traps. My interpretation of these technologies was built to a substantial extent on the excellent ethnographic work of English medical doctor and anthropologist Walter Roth, who was in the region in the 1890s and went on to become one of Queensland's first Aboriginal 'protectors' in 1898. But my knowledge was underpinned by what I had learnt about string, rope and net manufacture from the Lardil saltwater people of Mornington Island in the 1970s, who were one of the last Queensland groups to practise string-making. The local Georgina groups had been unable to maintain the skill due to the imposition of the *Aboriginal Protection Act* of 1897 and the consequent transformation of their economy.

In the mid-1970s at Gununa, or Mornington Island, I arranged with the Aboriginal Council to commission from the Old People the manufacture of a complete repertoire of customary artefacts from both the Lardil (North Wellesley Islands) and Kaiadilt (South Wellesley Islands) traditions to be housed in the University of Queensland's Anthropology Museum. Part of this production involved fibre collection; making, rolling, spinning and stranding strings and ropes; and the manufacture of various artefacts with the string, including nets.[5] The Lardil employed four types of fishing nets made from grass string, namely the hand-net or purse-net (*mijil*) to catch an individual fish chased from a rocky crevice, the elliptical scoop-net (*dumunthar*) for catching small fish and prawns

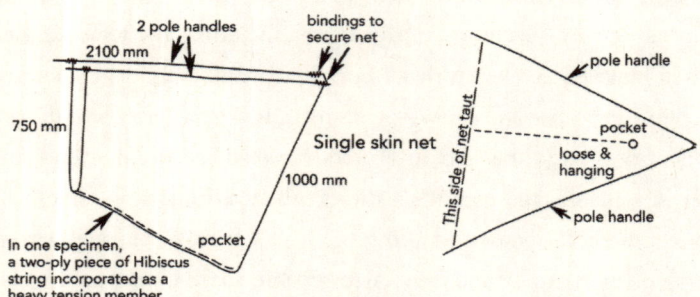

Side elevation – pole handles together   Plan – pole handles pulled wide apart

FIGURE 10: The Lardil *dulnhu kirra*, or grass-string net, used for catching *dulnhu* fish. Once fish are in the net, the poles are twisted inwards towards one another to close the mouth of the net.

from schools, and the *dulnhu kirra* (Figure 10) for catching fish in runs in channels and gutters. They also made a large two-handled dugong net (*larkuwen*) from rope manufactured from the bark of the yellow-flowered *Hibiscus tiliaceus* (*madard*), commonly called 'cotton tree' on the Queensland coast.

I was to encounter similar fibre technologies as I worked with different Aboriginal groups across the continent, and in various museum collections. The use of dugong nets set in the muddy bottom across channels involved a sizeable group of hunters in a cooperative team effort, with various men on rafts who would strategically chase a herd along a channel towards the nets, other men holding the net handles, and yet others to assist in drowning the dugong by holding their tails up and noses submerged. Obtaining three, four, five or six dugong in a successful hunt allowed a local clan to send messengers to invite many Lardil for a feast.

It is only in recent years that I have come to reflect more deeply on Aboriginal fibre technologies. One catalyst for this has been an international colleague, Swiss architectural anthropologist Nold Egenter, who has analysed what he terms the fibroconstructive industries of traditional societies, early humans, hominids and even primates as they developed and evolved nest building in association with defensive structures in their nocturnal camps, as the beginnings of an evolution of architecture. By fibroconstructive industries, Egenter means all manufacture with fibres – including grasses, vegetable fibres, plant stems, vines, canes, reeds and bamboos – in a broad sense, and many products (including simple and stranded strings and ropes), and techniques, including knotting, weaving, plaiting, thatching, binding, net-making, basketry, wickerwork, staked constructions and straw structures (for example, bound columns and towers). Egenter made me realise that fibroconstructive processes are a most widespread and long-lasting domain of human design enterprise, creativity and survival. Unfortunately, little remains of these biodegradable products in the archaeological evidence that researchers can access. A focused human history of the significance of the processes is therefore lacking, but Egenter's work forms an excellent introduction.

With these thoughts in mind, let us return to the Georgina River. Roth left us with some excellent ethnographic descriptions from the 1890s of the nets used, at times in conjunction with other devices, for trapping animals in the river basin.[6] It is normally dry for most of the year, but each wet season (December to April) the rivers fill and flow towards Lake Eyre. Then, as the dry commences, the flow diminishes, leaving the various perennial waterholes with fish, yabbies, edible waterlilies and many other resources.

Among the range of string fishing nets described by Roth, the largest were rectangular dragnets used in water that was waist to chest high in depth. Their length varied from 15 to 24 metres, their height was up to 2.1 metres, and they were often painted with bands of alternating red and yellow ochre. The largest were traded from the Maiawali people of the Diamantina River to the south-east. Figure 11(a) shows how a number of them were combined by a hunting group of twelve people to catch a school of yellowbelly or bream in the larger fullish waterholes, such as at Lake Francis.

Figure 11(b) shows a pair of strung rope nets for trapping ground animals, in particular kangaroos and emus. The overall width of the combined nets was 36 metres and the maximum height 2.1 metres. The nets were made of rope (similar to the dugong nets of the Lardil) of about 8 millimetres in diameter, knotted to form mesh rectangles of 30 × 22.5 centimetres. They were stretched across pathways into waterholes, or, if the pathways were too open, a V-shaped race or alleyway was made of a pair of foliage walls constructed by implanting or staking branches of foliage into lines of ground holes. Kangaroos were chased off the plains by hunters with dogs; emus could be attracted by the use of a didgeridoo imitating the

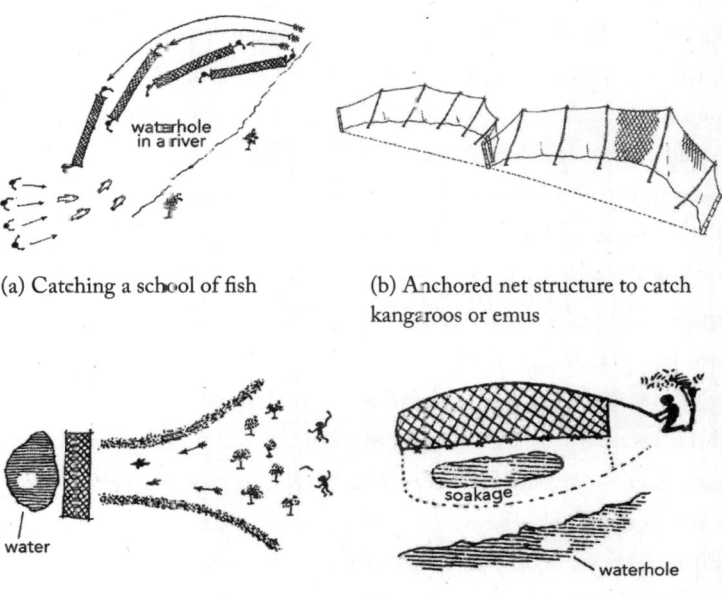

(a) Catching a school of fish

(b) Anchored net structure to catch kangaroos or emus

(c) Netting a flock of birds in a raceway (d) Netting birds at a soakage

FIGURE 1: Uses of net structures on the Georgina River recorded in the 1890s.

bird's drumming call. In sandy soil, emus were also caught using the call of the didgeridoo but with just a combination of foliage races and fences and excavated pitfalls.

The principle of the strung net – albeit string ones with a finer mesh – combined with the raceway or palisade could also be used to catch dozens or hundreds of small birds, such as budgerigars or parrots, which were chased out of trees by hunters using returning boomerangs and shrill calls to imitate hawk attacks, forcing them to fly low in their flocks, as shown in Figure 11(c).

Figure 11(d) illustrates another technique for catching flocks of pigeons, galahs or parrots adjacent to a large waterhole. Next to the main hole, clean water from the riverbed filters into a freshly hand-dug soakage. On the ground beside the soakage, a concealed hunter lays a long net that has a sapling handle along one side. The birds fly down to the clean soakage water (preferring it to the muddy water of the waterhole), even walking over the net and perhaps actually floating or bathing in the soakage. At an opportune moment, the hunter simply flips the net over using the handle in order to trap a number of birds underneath.

Roth also described fishing weirs at the end of the wet season when the river was still flowing but not too deep. A rock wall, used seasonally, is constructed across the river with several holes left in it to create gateways. The water spills through each of these holes into a circular depression enclosed by rocks and contains a net propped up with two sticks to form a bag that catches any fish that come through. This method was utilised by other riverine Aboriginal groups, the most sophisticated technological example of which is that utilised by several clans of Yolŋu people on the Glyde River in Arnhem Land, built of saplings and stringybark (see Figure 17 in Chapter 5).

VALUES IN SPINIFEX GRASS

In 1972, I met one of the few architects in Australia then undertaking a PhD, Peter Hamilton. He was married to Annette Hamilton, an anthropologist, and they had recently finished a year's fieldwork at Mimili in the central north of South Australia, where there was a semi-sedentary Yankunytjatjara camp of domed structures clad with spinifex grass. Peter was very knowledgeable on the architectural performance of the domes, having made meticulous records of their internal temperatures and responses to rainfall and strong desert winds. He concluded that they were very weatherproof and comfortable in the extremes of desert weather (cold, heat, dust storms). We spoke a lot about the insulation and rain-shedding properties of spinifex. He wrote two papers on the camp, mainly on its sociospatial properties and the social factors influencing the movement and reconstruction of domes, and then dropped out on the hippie trail, attending the Aquarius Festival in Nimbin in 1973 and joining one of the first communes in that part of northern New South Wales, where he remained until old age.

In the years leading to his death, Peter asked me to try to retrieve his unique records from Sydney University and gave me permission to use his photos of dome construction in my book *Gunyah, Goondie + Wurley*. My colleague Carroll Go-Sam, a Dyirbal scholar, co-authored the chapter titled 'Spinifex Domes of the Western Desert'. After the book was published, an opportunity arose to look more closely at Aboriginal knowledge and uses of spinifex grass. I was ten years into developing a friendship with an Aboriginal leader, Colin Saltmere, from Camooweal. Colin – whom I address by his skin name, Pwerle – and I brainstormed the ingredients for a potential grant application to the Australian Government, and I returned to Queensland University to assemble a team of Indjalandji and Alyawarr elders, an architect, a botanist, an archaeologist, a bionanotechnology engineer, a chemist, an ecologist and an anthropologist (me). This transdisciplinary team analysed the properties of spinifex grass and recorded many findings, including the traditional uses of the grass as cladding (as instructed by Ruby Saltmere, Pwerle's mother) and of the grass's sticky resin to make medicines and gums for hafting stone blades. We also looked into novel modern uses and practical applications for the grass and its ingredients.[7]

There are sixty or more species of prickly, undervalued spinifex hummock grasses growing across a third of the continent, and the wide range of uses our team uncovered in the traditional material cultures of many Aboriginal groups[8] inspired us. We were looking for local low-tech applications that could be used by Aboriginal communities in Central Australia, and to this end studied bough shed roofs, insulation batts of compressed grass, spinifex-reinforced adobe walls and slabs, and use of the resin as a timber coating to provide durability and protect from white-ant attack. We also searched for novel high-tech applications that could command a good price in international markets. Our team of bionano engineers explored the many physical and chemical properties of *Triodia pungens*, a species that grows in abundance in the Georgina Basin. This species has two sacred sites in the basin area, each with its own Dreaming history that underpins the traditional owners' interests and values, and provides a mandate for the project based in Aboriginal law.

After five years, our project grant[9] was beginning to run out when a junior team member, Nasim Amiralian (a chemical engineer from Iran), made a breakthrough by discovering the significance of the grass's nanofibres. Grass fibres break down into smaller and smaller fibrils until they reach the nanoscale; one nanofibre is invisible to the naked eye. Nasim discovered that the nanofibres had a very high tensile strength, commensurate with that of steel. If they could be extracted without expensive chemicals or pollutant by-products, they could then be remixed with other biodegradable components to make new materials with very high strength. Since that discovery, many such products have been explored and have attracted commercial interest. For example, the Malaysian rubber industry has added the nanofibres to surgical gloves and condoms to strengthen them. Other manufacturers have added them to recycled paper and cardboard to make high-strength packaging, or included them in forms of concrete to eliminate steel reinforcement. Work is now underway on the potential role of nano additives in repairing parts of the human body.

Buoyed by our progress, Pwerle secured appropriate recognition and intellectual property control over the Aboriginal knowledge component through brokered agreements with the university. He also strongly influenced the Queensland Government to reform and amend its *Biodiscovery Act* (2004) to assist Aboriginal traditional owner groups to establish commercially viable enterprises. And he raised funding to construct a bioprocessing plant in the Dugalunji Camp. Installed in the plant is a $600,000 supercritical carbon dioxide condenser from Switzerland that extracts and separates the fibres, resins, oils and other grass products for different uses, as well as an elaborate set of spinifex grass cutting and baling equipment. The aim is to start a new industry for remote Aboriginal Australia, with franchises or similar for outstation and community groups to harvest and provide product and perhaps then establish their own bioprocessing plants as the market grows.

This is Aboriginal engineering – with supportive collaborators – at its best. From the Dreaming to the market! Its goal is to establish meaningful employment, enterprise and hope in the bush and simultaneously strengthen Indigenous identities around the customary values of engineering – transforming from the macro to the nano.

ASSEMBLING SYMBOLIC AND RITUAL PLACES

The Dreaming is clearly important in understanding Aboriginal design, engineering and architecture. However, it might be surprising to learn that the most elaborate and symbolic places could be dismantled and erased after one short use. Most people today know little about ceremonial grounds that were ritual theatres for enacting sacred religious knowledge. This knowledge was often restricted either along gender lines or by degrees of initiation, although there were and still are various public ceremonies. Only a relatively small number of Aboriginal groups practise traditional ceremonies with highly embellished grounds; for most, the knowledge has been lost. In Chapter 7, Alison writes of the scope for reinvention of ceremony in contemporary urban settings.

I have had the good fortune and privilege of witnessing – and indeed participating in, in a limited way – ceremonies in the Gulf of Carpentaria and Central Australia, partly through assisting groups to re-perform and revitalise ceremonies that had been suppressed and stopped by missionaries some fifty or sixty years previously, and partly in my role as an expert-witness anthropologist assisting with land claims in the Northern Territory. Most recently, knowledge was shared with me by an outback town group who wanted to educate white townspeople on why ceremony time had to be respected and due allowance made for ceremonial duties by the town's service agencies.

Traditional ceremonial leaders are knowledgeable men and women of the highest esteem who have indelibly remembered, through years of teaching and performance, all of the design ingredients necessary to orchestrate many different ceremonies. These details encompass selecting the appropriate ground and time of performance, conscripting necessary governance support, requisitioning a cast of performers of appropriate levels of initiation and totemic identities, assembling all necessary raw materials and food supplies, constructing specially designed sculptures and ground/body/artefact paintings, supervising the performance and accuracy of the choreography, leading the performance through singing the appropriate songs, and ensuring the dismantling and erasure of all secret aspects afterwards. All of this has to be done exactly the way it has been done forever, passed down through the generations from the ancestors of the Dreaming. The design of the ceremonial ground contains symbolic maps of Country, and the songs and performances re-enact the sacred histories of particular Dreaming ancestors. Painstaking energy and ritual procedure are invested in these performances, and violation of the ground is the ultimate sacrilege.

Combinations of earth sculptures, freestanding painted and otherwise decorated sculptures of organic materials (often containing sacred objects), and shelters are assembled on ritual grounds to generate forms of symbolic ceremonial architecture. A relatively equitable social status exists among elders of the same generation given the exigencies of personality, specialist occupation and personal interests in the various cultural domains of life. This is despite certain elders in Aboriginal groups filling various offices of public duty, such as senior estate custodian, senior ceremonial leader or songman, doctor, surgeon, messenger, peacemaker – the list goes on.

There was thus no social hierarchy or wealth accumulation in the make-up of Aboriginal Australia that might have led to elaborate residences, some more pretentious or grand than others, such as the chief's houses and men's houses to be found in New Guinea and elsewhere in Melanesia.[10] An exception for some groups was evident in forms of structures to farewell and/or store the dead. These included graves with mounds (sometimes inside huts), platforms and cylindrical bark coffins in caves, embellished in different ways with symbolic markers, including feathers, bones, painted wooden structures, cylindrical stones, incised bark, carved tree trunks, the deceased's possessions, or firewood for use at reincarnation.[11]

A mode of burial seen in the Barka or lower Darling River area in the late 19th century demonstrates the impressive extent of skill and technological detail that could be invested in such a special architectural work:

> Should the person buried have been esteemed of consideration prior to death a neat hut is erected over the grave, the covering thereof being generally thatch, made of a hard knotty bark, having many joints, probably, therefore, akin to polygonum [lignum]. This thatch is firmly secured to the frame by cord, many hundred yards of which are used in the work.
>
> On some occasions a net is made, having meshes 4 inches [100 mm] square, with which the hut is completely enveloped.
>
> These mausoleums cover the grave entirely; they are about 5 feet [1.5 metres] high, and are of an oval shape; a small opening or doorway is left at the eastern end; these openings are never more than 30 inches [750 mm] high, only being large enough to allow of a full grown man creeping in; the tops of the graves or floors of the huts are covered with grass, which is renewed from time to time as it becomes withered. The tombs are enclosed by brush fencing, the forms of the enclosures being of a diamond-shape; the tomb in every instance is exactly in the centre; all the grass inside of the fence is neatly shaved off, and the ground swept quite clean.[12]

Complex architectural symbolism was a result of the preoccupation with cosmology (Dreaming beliefs) and cosmogony (the origin of the universe and our place within it). In contrast, only some groups appear to have attached symbolism to shelters. However, particular forms or designs or components of a shelter did carry particular meanings in certain Aboriginal groups. Relationships between Aboriginal cosmologies and different types of dwellings can be illustrated for various groups in northern and central Australia. One such sacred history of the Eastern Arrernte (formerly spelt Aranda) people concerns the construction technology of a wet-weather shelter, related by the late Walter Smith Purula from the Simpson Desert. The location, Arrabarre, is near the upper Marshall River, a tributary of the Plenty River that flows into the Simpson Desert.[13]

In the Altjira, the Dreaming, no-one knew how to make shelters. The men of [Arrabarre] held a meeting. They decided to visit a man of great wisdom who lived a short distance to the east, for they thought he would know how to keep warm and dry when the storms came. The middle-aged men of authority decided that a boy should travel with them, even though the journey was strictly for initiated men, for the law would have to be passed on for generation after generation. Thus it was that they chose an intelligent youth to travel with them, and they set out … They found the wise man at his home upon a mountain peak, and he was indeed the keeper of the law of the storm shelter. He showed them how to erect a framework then, most important of all, indicated how the branches must be placed over it so that leaf fingers overlapped leaf fingers. Now, when it rained, the water could not penetrate the shelter … The men then returned to their great eastern Aranda rain centre and taught the women the necessary skills. That is how the law of the rainproof shelters was established. From that time on men were obliged to perform the rain ceremonies correctly and to keep secret from women certain dangerous knowledge connected with the learning about shelter construction. In return the women reciprocated by assisting to build the shelters and were obliged to collect the firewood needed to keep the families warm.[14]

This indicates that there was further sacred knowledge linked to the wet-weather shelter that was of a restrictive nature and so generated further cosmological dimensions.

Linguists who have asked about the literal meanings and etymology of words used for naming houses or shelters and their constituent structural and cladding components have discovered that they have a range of meanings. For a number of the Arnhem Land domestic shelters recorded, the anthropologist Donald Thomson investigated various names in different languages in the mid-20th century, particularly the domed mosquito house, horizontal timber platform and stringybark-clad vaults (supported and unsupported). He found that the names for the dome-shaped mosquito house, *liya-damala* and *gilkal*, translated to 'head of the eagle/eagle's nest' and 'moon' respectively in different Yolŋu languages, while the stringybark barrel vaults and double-ridgepole vaulted structures were consistently called *dhudi djirikitj* (meaning 'quail's nest') when they had one end open and one shut, and *durara marma* ('two mouths') when they had both ends open.[15] The Djirikitj or ancestral quail is also closely associated with the Gumatj clan's ancestral fire history. In this story, a 'sacred shade' containing sacred Yolŋu objects catches fire. The quail picks up a lighted twig from the burning shelter and drops it into the dry grass, spreading fire across the country and thereby burning off.[16] There is an implicit implication here that the Dreaming energy or essence from the shelter was absorbed into the fire and spread through Country.

5

MATERIALS

ADAPTATION AND MATERIALS

ALISON PAGE

If necessity is the mother of invention, then it naturally flows that Indigenous people, who have survived in some of the harshest conditions over major climatic changes, must be inherently innovative and adaptable. At the start of the Last Glacial Period (or Ice Age), which is the most significant climatic event ever faced by humans on this continent, as much as 80 per cent of Australia was temporarily abandoned by Aboriginal people.[1] They altered and adapted their lifestyles to survive, which even extended to the alteration of their spiritual beliefs and cultural narratives to accommodate these necessary changes. But they never 'abandoned' their homelands and stories completely. Some fishers in Arnhem Land still observe the land boundaries in the sea that existed during the Ice Age, in case the seas retreat once again and the protocols around tribal boundaries need to be observed. The decision to maintain lifestyles built around the climatic rhythms of the land and sea speaks of a culture that is clever, adaptive and inventive.

When I was a kid, one of the most popular shows on television was *Bush Mechanics*. It's a humorous series set in Central Australia about fellas from the Warlpiri community of Yuendumu who are smart problem-solvers, repairing their clapped-out cars with bush solutions. One of the most memorable episodes for me was when a flat tyre was fixed by stuffing it with spinifex; the gang were back on the road within ten minutes.

Upcycling and adaptive re-use were commonplace in Indigenous households when I was growing up. My friend Phil Duncan took me to his uncle's house in Moree for a barbecue and demonstrated a pressure cooker that his uncle had made from a beer keg. He had carved it horizontally and added clips and rubber rings to seal in the air. Inside, custom-made shelves ensured that vegetables and yellowbelly fish could be cooked to perfection on various levels.

Two principles are at work in this creative process. The first is lateral thinking in the formation of ideas, and the second is adaptive re-use of discarded materials. It is this second principle that I want to explore further and highlight how it relates to the Indigenous approach to using materials.

For thousands of years, Indigenous people have lived in a materially rich culture, with boomerangs shaped and carved from carefully chosen hardwoods, dillybags and fish traps woven from finely twisted fibres, and tools skilfully knapped by applying exact pressure on a piece of stone. Part of the Indigenous relationship to Country is fully understanding the resources available to provide shelter, food, tools and medicines. That understanding is deeply rooted in the organisation of the landscape and its materials into kinship networks, totemic systems, moieties (social or ritual groups into which a community is divided) and areas of responsibility. All those materials – wood, stone, string, resin – were harvested from plants that have a multidimensional relationship with people. These relationships are embedded into the social structures to ensure the ongoing care and maintenance of the plants and their materials. For instance, the wattle not only provides wood for carving and making tools, it is also a medicine and food and a seasonal indicator, letting you know when the mullet are running. The responsibility to maintain this knowledge is owned by the family group whose plant totem is the wattle.

As we have described, materials are viewed as products of the bodies and deeds of the ancestors, elaborately described in Dreaming stories. As objects were traded along the Songlines from hand to hand, Country to Country, they carried with them the essence and spirit of the ancestors, which is where the origins of these 'living' objects lie. This is why materials have always been inseparable from spirituality, and why anyone who harvests botanical material must ask permission of the plant or tree before taking from it. My cousin

Dean Kelly, a Yuin man and ranger, taught me to stand in front of the tree or bush and place my bare feet on the ground, tell the bush I am coming and that I am here to ask if I can take these leaves. When you are deeply connected to Country and able to listen, you will hear the answer to the question. It may be 'No', in which case you have to find another tree that is willing to give.

In the mid-20th century, east of Bunnerong Road in Sydney, builders were excavating for a sewerage system extension. Under about 10.5 metres of earth they discovered a boomerang, later identified as one of the oldest found in New South Wales, that would have been a beloved artefact of one of the traditional owners who occupied the sandy dunes in Sydney's south-east. What was curious about it was the way the object had been modified: a steel collar had been added to reinforce its centre. It was a well-worn object with chipped edges, so the retrofitting of the stronger material would have been like breathing years of life into it so it could last longer. The metal is a skilfully applied piece of sheeting that is curled around the edges of the boomerang, just in the centre, suggesting that the owner must have appreciated its value and wanted to extend the life of this family member.

How does such incorporation of human-made additions fit within the spiritual philosophy of objects and materials? In his book *Ochre and Rust*, Philip Jones suggests, in regard to analysing the addition of metal to stone axes, that 'the Aboriginal relationship to this new substance is poorly understood'.[2] What we do know is that the adoption of new materials was taken up by the people but that it somewhat disrupted the social order. Jones describes the observations of anthropologist Lauriston Sharp when he was conducting fieldwork with the Yir Yoront people in the 1940s. Sharp saw how metal axes upset a tightly controlled social order relating to the access to and ownership of these precious tools traditionally made of stone and wood:

> Stone axes were not just inefficient tools, to be readily abandoned in favour of metal; they were key social markers, which helped to articulate the mechanism of Yir Yoront society ... A sudden surfeit of metal axes during the 1940s, equally available to all members of Yir Yoront society, represented a direct assault on this tense and delicate order: women and uninitiated boys now had ready access to a tool which had previously been carefully regulated. But Sharp's analysis suggests that even if the Yir Yoront realised the corrosive social effect of this new commodity, the metal's efficacy made it irresistible.[3]

It is highly likely that spiritual beliefs and social structures were adapted to accommodate new materials as they were so widely traded. Jones remarks that:

> stone tools were regarded as exotic items, such as at a central Simpson Desert site visited by this author, many kilometres from any source of stone, where unblemished edge-ground axe-heads mark three separate burials. Undoubtedly, metal axes also entered this sacred domain.[4]

The foreign materials that appeared at the time of the first encounters with the colonisers were so quickly adopted into artefact making and traded across the country that some arrived in particular areas before white people did.

Said to be the pinnacle of stone-tool craftsmanship, the Kimberley points, as they became known, are finely flaked glass spearpoints from the Kimberley region of Western Australia. They were often made from glass bottles or ceramic telegraph-wire insulators instead of stone, and their continual use as spearheads was noted from the early 19th century onwards. They became prized for their functionality, as anthropologist Kim Akerman wrote:

> Both glass and stone points not only penetrate but also have the added advantage over wooden spearheads of promoting haemorrhage. If these points separate from the fore-shaft or break while in the body of a target, they act as shrapnel, which further enhances their efficacy.[5]

Glass points were also easier to repair and manufacture, in that they broke effortlessly from their mounting and could be quickly remounted and used again. And the glass was more easily worked than stone, so they could be quickly manufactured.

As the points were traded along Songlines from their origin in the Kimberley, they took on a spiritual significance to the surrounding tribal groups. Akerman noted that 'In terms of perceived metaphysical powers, large glass points were regarded in the Central Australian and Western Desert areas … as potent symbols of lightning and rain and were eagerly sought – not only for their aesthetic appeal, but also for use as ritual knives.'[6]

As more materials – from corrugated iron to cloth and canvas – infiltrated the world of Indigenous people, the designs of artefacts and the stories that accompanied them adapted. The decisions for this adaptation, while driven by efficacy and functionality, still needed to accommodate cultural requirements.

For millennia, Indigenous people decided for the most part not to advance their technologies beyond fibre, stone, ochre and wood, which meant that they were classified by Western scientists as a 'primitive' civilisation. However, it is more likely in hindsight that they possessed an advanced thinking around maintaining flexible living practices. I have often wondered whether mud was once thrown into a fire but the resulting clay rejected because of its weight and effect on making life more sedentary, reducing the chances of survival.

In a way, the knowledge of the land and climate and the necessary movement and flexibility have continued into Indigenous design and cultural practices, perhaps as a hangover from the Last Glacial Period. Aboriginal and Torres Strait Islander peoples are renowned the world over for their adoption of contemporary styles of cultural expression, and they proudly own the title of the world's oldest 'living' culture. Now that we are coming to terms with the finality of the earth's resources, perhaps we should be reassessing what is 'primitive' and what is 'advanced'. When we are at the drawing board, making decisions to improve our society, we need to look back to look forward. In traditional society, technology progressed only if it met the balance of improving efficiency, maintaining culture and protecting Country. This delicate balance of values begins to build the basis of what we can define as our Indigenous design principles. But more on that in Chapter 8.

A DEEPER CONSIDERATION OF ARTEFACTS AND THEIR DESIGN ATTRIBUTES

PAUL MEMMOTT

The properties of artefacts include their design and manufacture, materials and form, appearance and decoration, use and storage, meanings and symbolism, and whether particular objects are unique or of one-off design or made in multiple copies, whether by artisans or machines.

We can also consider categories or families of artefacts, where individual objects have a natural association with one another. For example, we could consider the items that are typically found in a restaurant kitchen, or in a Lardil dugong-hunting camp. Some categories of artefacts are specific to particular cultural or subcultural groups, such as courtroom judges and lawyers, Catholic nuns or Yolŋu goose-egg hunters in Arnhem Land.

Today, many artefacts spread very quickly around the world due to the processes of globalisation driven by mass media and international trade. One aspect of the properties of artefacts is how they come into a cultural group's possession. They can arrive by local invention, by being traded or purchased from another place or group, or by being copied and perhaps modified and adapted for local use.

When new artefacts – or for that matter new ideas or customs – are spreading across a continent or around the world and are being relatively freely accepted, anthropologists use the terms 'diffusion' and 'indirect change'. When the British arrived in Australia, various Aboriginal artefacts, technologies and customs were diffusing across the continent from clan to clan. In contrast to indirect change, if a new object is imposed by force on a cultural group or an old object is removed from a cultural group by an invading army or a dictatorship or a government, the process is termed 'directed change'. This is what occurred when the colonial administrations took control of many Aboriginal people and imposed rules about wearing clothes, living in permanent work camps, and adapting to new technologies and foods.

In 2020, in response to the coronavirus, the Victorian Government imposed a rule, punishable by monetary fine, stating that all citizens must wear a face mask when in public. Some people resisted and were fined. By contrast, not so long ago in Australia, due to fear of terrorist attacks certain people were campaigning against Muslim women covering their faces in public with forms of hijab (the niqab and burka). Here we see different social values about the use (or misuse) of certain artefacts being employed in particular cultural contexts. Obtaining a new artefact, or changing the pattern of customary use of it, does not necessarily happen easily. The process of change can involve the steps of intelligent appreciation of the artefact's potential use or misuse (gun bans come to mind), whether it can be accepted, what the impacts and costs will be, and the decision to trade or buy and then use the artefact (for example, will I buy the latest smartphone?).

WELLESLEY ISLANDS MATERIAL CULTURE AND
SPECIALISATION OF ARTEFACTS

In the 1970s, when the Anthropology Museum at the University of Queensland (UQ) engaged me to commission the respective sets of artefacts used by the Lardil people (North Wellesley Islands) and the Kaiadilt people (South Wellesley Islands), interesting questions arose as to why there were lots of similarities but also many differences between the two sets.[7] Although it is an immense task to reconstruct millennia of evolutionary developments in material culture, there existed a challenging opportunity to conduct such a study. The questions about the local evolution of material culture could be broadened by examining the other language groups of the Wellesley Islands.

The Yanggal, who formed the trading link between the Lardil and the mainland coast, had a material culture identical to that of the Lardil. However, the material culture of the Kaiadilt people of the South Wellesley Islands had several differences from that of the Lardil. The southern islands have a similar environment to that of the North Wellesleys, but the Lardil had a repertoire of some sixty-five or more artefacts, while the Kaiadilt repertoire numbered around thirty.[8] Two items in the Kaiadilt repertoire were not found among the Lardil, and a number were used for the same purpose by both groups but differed in their design. Artefacts in common included the raft, paddle, bark torch, shell knife, stone oyster hammer, spearthrower, bark dish, fighting stick, firesticks and small hand-nets. Both groups also used rock-wall fish traps. Lardil artefacts with no

Kaiadilt equivalent included the dugong net, large fishing nets, the message stick, the handball, septum ornaments and dance artefacts. Conversely, several items in the Kaiadilt repertoire were not found among the Lardil. One was a weapon, a round-shafted throwing stick (*jadiyeli*) made from a *Terminalia* species (*dankaburrd*), with each end sharpened into a narrow prong. The Kaiadilt hunting (*muurraj*) and fishing (*kurumbu*) spears had much larger heads and prongs respectively and bore more numerous timber barbs than their Lardil counterparts. The Kaiadilt also had a specialised form of hunting spear (*kujiji*) up to 3.3 metres long, which had a two-piece shaft and a separate head.[9]

How could such differences exist at the same time as the many commonalities? The research my colleagues and I undertook indicates that the two groups innovated different methods of dealing intellectually and technologically with everyday problems and concerns, resulting in differences in the simplicity, complexity, diversity and extent of their daily objects despite similar environments. The design of the set of artefacts was as important as the design of each individual artefact, if not more so. With this understanding, we can see why Aboriginal artefacts differ all over the continent but many groups share common categories or styles of artefacts. This is not surprising given the pervasive trade routes, but people's local needs and values decided which type and style were most suitable or acceptable in their local context.

One of the hypotheses my research colleagues and I worked with is that over the last three or four millennia, the Kaiadilt chose to expand the quantity of rock-wall fish traps they built and embellish the combinations and permutations of the traps for different annual and lunar tidal contexts, as well as design strong spearheads to kill dugong and turtles inside the traps. In contrast, the Lardil preferred to strengthen their internal social networks to enable larger group hunts for dugong and turtle and fishing hauls using nets as well as rafts, rather than relying exclusively on rock-wall fish traps. For the Lardil, fibre engineering (net technology) won out over fish farming in variable tidal regimes. The Lardil were also open to trade with their neighbours, at times receiving new ideas from the mainland. However, the Kaiadilt preferred their insularity and resisted much of the change diffusing along the coast despite occasional visits there, preferring their own local design inventions.

TRADE OF ARTEFACTS: DESIGN IN THE DREAMING

In 1939, the anthropologist Fred McCarthy of the Australian Museum in Sydney published an enlightening sequence of papers analysing how trade operated in Aboriginal Australia. By examining the reports of many other anthropologists, he was able to map the dominant trade routes across the continent and connections to New Guinea and Indonesia (see Figure 12). Some were so prolific that they were essentially trunk trade routes, such as the one that lay along the Georgina River, passed through Camooweal, connected to the Gulf of Carpentaria to the north, and passed to the south around Lake Eyre and through the Flinders Ranges to the south coast. This trade route was still functioning on the Georgina in the early 1890s even though colonial pastoralists had been in the region since the 1860s, and was well recorded then by Walter Roth, who found that there were established trading markets at the large perennial waterholes on the river and identified the different flows of artefacts in and out of the region. Many of the trade routes linking the perennial water sources followed the travel routes of the Dreaming ancestors who created those sites (linked in the Songlines), and travelling traders of the appropriate totem were guaranteed security and safety on those routes.[10]

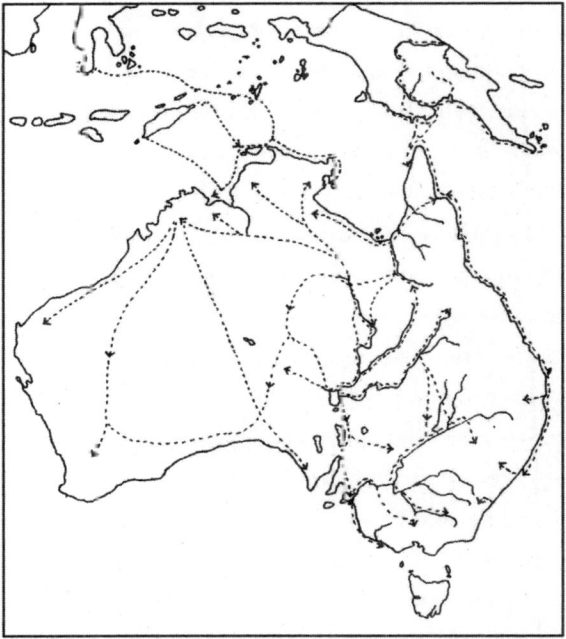

FIGURE 12: The Aboriginal trunk trading routes that operated throughout the Australian mainland and beyond at the time of European settlement, as analysed by FD McCarthy.[11]

People travelled from all directions to these markets to obtain things they needed. For various reasons, certain objects were in high demand on the trade routes. Perhaps a particular material was not available locally, and produce made from that material had to be imported. Looking at the example of Lake Francis on the Georgina River at Camooweal, we find that there is no sandstone anywhere in the local region and so large, flat slabs of sandstone were imported for grindstone bases from the Wangkamanha (or Wongkamala) people of the Toko Range on the eastern side of the Simpson Desert far to the south, near an extension of the Georgina named Mulligan Creek. Here among the sand dunes was the relatively small plant that scientists today call *Duboisia hopwoodii*, whose common Aboriginal name is *pituri*. Its fried leaves provided a strong drug that was packed into distinctive, tightly woven ornate and coloured pituri string bags specially designed for the purpose of long-distance travel and trade. One in the Queensland Museum was obtained at Burketown near the southern coast of the Gulf of Carpentaria. In the vicinity of this northern point on the trade route, shells arrived from around the coast on their way inland to the desert nations, where they were greatly valued and used as an emblem of manhood presented to young men when they underwent a stage of their initiation ceremony, tied around their waist as a pubic pendant. I have seen decorated pearl shells in Central Australia that were traded from around Broome through the desert routes. All of these shells were pierced with a small hole for tying as a pendant of some sort.

At Lake Francis we find another imported item (not available locally) in the greenstone hand-axes made of an igneous rock and used for chopping into trees to extract the much-loved honey of the wild bees, or for breaking out timber slabs from certain acacia trees to manufacture boomerangs. The axes came from the Kalkatungu people in the highlands to the east around what is now Mount Isa. The Kalkatungu were stonemason specialists, having access to igneous and metamorphic rocks in the rich, mountainous geological field where there are now many commercial mines. For them, certain types of stone and the artefacts they produced were actual Dreamings.

However, the Indjalandji at Lake Francis and surrounds were not without their own stone production. On the blacksoil plains of the surrounding tableland country are many outcrops of a fine-grained banded chert known locally as ribbon stone, from which blades of various sizes were manufactured for meat-butchering knives, spearheads, chisels, surgical blades and other uses. McCarthy reported that chisel blades were in high demand because the manufacturing of timber shields and coolamons (carrying vessels) and the preparation of fluted boomerangs necessitated frequent replacement of blades. The timber handle was retained and a bag of blades would be obtained, as well as a supply of the best spinifex gum for hafting blade to handle. (Spinifex was another resource that was a Dreaming in its own right.)

In a recent heritage survey along the path of a gas pipeline development running east–west across the upper Georgina Basin, Indjalandji rangers and elders found one chert quarry site, among many smaller ones, that was estimated at 13 kilometres long and over 4 kilometres wide. Almost every eligible stone had been worked over and cracked open in the search for good blade material. I have travelled across these plains of the Barkly Tableland for some four decades noting the innumerable quarries, but it has only been in the last two decades that I've had the privilege of travelling with Colin Saltmere Pwerle, one of the last stonemasons or knappers in Aboriginal Australia searching these quarries. He goes there to source good-quality stones from which to release multiple blades with perfect cleavage, using minimal blows with his hammer stone. On one memorable trip, we went to an aesthetically impressive pure white outcrop protruding intermittently above the surface over some 50 or more kilometres. This stone had a most spiritual quality – and here is a revelation about the trade system: the most sought-after items had spiritual or magical qualities left from the Dreaming, and the purchaser believed that these qualities provided the items with enhanced capacities.

This phenomenon was well reported by McCarthy in his continental survey of trade. For example, he wrote that 'One of the wandering ancestral groups named what is now called Mt Sonder Urachipma, or the place of the pitchi, because here they found an old bandicoot man engaged in making them.' His point was that the localities of where the most prized artefacts came from were where the Ancestral Beings of the Dreaming first invented, designed and manufactured them; and that in such localities the artefact forms a Dreaming or totem now held by the local group, who believe they are descended from the original Ancestral Beings. Another example cited by McCarthy is the Red Ochre Dreaming from the prized ochre quarries at and near Parachilna in Adnyamathanha (or Atnyamatna) Country in the Flinders Ranges, north of Adelaide. This ochre also made its way north to the Georgina trade route, passing around Lake Eyre, as did the most prized obsidian (volcanic green glass) from western Victoria.

The spiritual property of an artefact would be even more potent if the manufacturer was not only of the appropriate totemic identity but could also 'sing' or 'talk' to the artefact during manufacture using a song or speech protocol believed to be part of the sacred history associated with the Dreaming. For example, in Chapter 2, Alison describes Frank Gurrmanamana from Djunawunya in Arnhem Land singing and talking to a fish trap as he is making it; and I have written of Jackson Jacob from Mornington Island, who outlined to me the importance of talking in Lardil to Thuwathu, the Rainbow Serpent, as he extracted the slab of boomerang timber from a kurrburu tree to appease the ancestor and ensure his spirit was imbued in the final shaped object. McCarthy pointed out that such artisans would accrue a reputation based on the spiritual quality of their artefacts that was in addition to their skill reputation in the technical manufacturing process, and that in later life they would have a relative degree of wealth and abundance of food due to their command of the trading markets. Their reputable wares, replete with designer song patented from the Dreaming, would be traded far across the continent. Hence the diffusion of pearl shell and other magical objects from northern coastal areas into the deserts.

NEGOTIATING CHANGE

Reflecting on the differences between the sets of Lardil and Kaiadilt artefacts, we can recognise significant processes of cultural change occurring. The Kaiadilt expanded, refined and embellished their rock-wall trap technology while simultaneously acknowledging the function of large-net technology, but nevertheless decided in the main to reject those nets. Why? Perhaps the reason was to do with the Lardil being more willing and able to negotiate among themselves in forming large hunting parties drawn from different clan groups to cooperate on dugong hunts.

This brings us to creative decision-making in classical Aboriginal societies and how it might have worked in relation to inventing or innovating new designs. What must first of all be emphasised is the inherent conservatism of Aboriginal traditional belief systems and the people's innate resistance to changing fundamental aspects of culture. When I travelled with Alyawarr elders working on land claims and recording sacred sites for protection during the 1980s and early 90s, I witnessed many lengthy and sometimes intense debates focused on 'straightening' knowledge and authenticating customary knowledge. My teacher Albert Morton would insist it had to be *arretye*, straight! The Law had to be kept straight. He would say, 'Don't make a mistake when using totemic ceremonial symbols. If you wear another man's paint, you'll be six foot under!'

In the 1970s, the musicologist Richard Moyle, who had worked with the Alyawarr recording all their ceremonial songs under the tutorage of Albert and his elder brothers, wrote:

[Alyawarr songs] ... are held to have been transmitted faithfully and with total accuracy through numberless generations to the extent that they have the status of an ultimate authority in matters of ceremonial detail or in what are considered historical facts ... Also included as indispensable and unchanging are the order of ceremonial events ... the timing of performances, and the various responsibilities and social relationships existing among the participants ... [These] elements of ceremonial life ... came from the Dreamtime and have been faithfully perpetuated by successive generations of ancestors and must continue in the same manner.[12]

Here is part of the secret of the perpetuation of the society and the permanency of the sustainable relationship with the environment over millennia. The ceremonies kept descent groups bound to local places through belief in totemic affiliation, ritual responsibility and being of and from the Dreaming. As Ted Strehlow observed, these inviolable connections prevented the idea of conquering large tracts of country by any one group, for the conquerors would neither have the correct ritual knowledge nor be in the appropriate totemic relation to manifest it in other foreign lands. Descent groups thus maintained longstanding custodianship and ritual relations to their local Countries. When compared to our global society today, change in the old Australia occurred only slowly, and in many instances took many generations. Anthropologists and linguists have studied how certain customs and language traits gradually diffused and were locally adapted, where feasible, into local conservative frameworks of the Law. But such slow processes could be disrupted by acute environmental change – for example, extreme periods of drought in the interior or changing sea levels on the coast, perhaps in the form of tsunamis. Then groups had to migrate and seek refuge in other peoples' countries, with possible clashes and collisions of rights and customs.[13] Adaptations then had to be made.

During the 1970s, I worked intensively with a cross-section of about ten male elders of the Lardil from across the four main geographic divisions of their society. They were the knowledge holders and songmen, and they were my teachers. After a decade I could confidently write about how some of them were extremely conservative. For them, true knowledge came from Country and from the Dreaming, and was either handed down from father and father's father on one's clan Country; or came as gifts of knowledge encoded in songs from the spirit forms of ancestors at sacred sites on Country, literally in the Dreaming, and transmitted through dreams. All the Lardil songs with their dances, body designs and actions had been dreamt in this way. The northern songmen had their dances dreamt at their sites, the southern songmen had their dances, and so on for those in the east and west. One of the conservative elders was old Fred, a southern songman I write about in Chapter 7, and whom I was with when he dreamt a new dance one night while we were camping.

There was another category of elders whom I called the 'creatives', or, we could say here, the 'designers'. They too believed in old Law, dreamt songs and passed those songs down their family lines. But in addition they interrogated this body of knowledge in a critical way, similar to how a Western scientist might in a paper in a science journal. They recognised gaps in the knowledge, formulated hypotheses on how those gaps might be filled, and creatively sought solutions. Where dreamt knowledge was not coherent, they pieced together bits of different people's dreams and creatively inserted new ideas where explanation was wanting. In presenting their knowledges – whether it be dance renditions, geographic knowledge, sacred histories or object design – they were always challenged by the conservative elders. But over their lifetime the creatives sometimes won out in seeding new ideas, introducing changes in the way things were done, or teaching younger adults new pathways of traditions. There was always a tension in the society between these opposing forces, designer versus conservative, change versus no change, and adaptation sometimes won out. Let us consider a couple of instances of this, although I must be careful as some resulted in painful conflicts that I can't discuss here.

In the early mission period, the missionaries encouraged men to adapt their customary bark technology for new cottage walls and roof cladding. Messmate bark was stripped, heated and smoked over a low fire, then flattened with heavy stones and cut into rectangular sheets for cladding. My *kantha* (adoptive father), Burrud, worked on the mission sailing boats that transported goods to communities around the Gulf, and he saw bark paintings in eastern Arnhem Land. Burrud was a leading creative elder and decided to implement his own art style. First, he simply replicated on pieces of flattened bark his totemic body designs used in dancing. In some he used the chopped-up feather down that was traditionally adhered to the body with human blood. Then he painted designs onto the bark showing scenes and artefacts of traditional life. He innovated further in one painting by fusing an abstract image of Thuwathu into a stylised map of the Country through which this Ancestral Being travelled. By the late 1950s, both Burrud and his younger brother Goobalathaldin

(Dick) were painting Lardil sacred histories from the Larumbenda (south division), including stories about animals from the Dreaming and about the first humans who created the coastal places in the geography. However, in the backgrounds to these story renditions they repeatedly used decorative crosshatching, which they 'borrowed' from the Arnhem Land style of painting – a borrowing that was severely criticised by many. The criticism did not last and other younger men eventually followed in their footsteps and the paintings were exported to the Aboriginal art and craft market. More and more adults of the community took up and replicated their style, but without trying any innovation, to supplement their incomes. The style, known as the Mornington Island art style, persisted in a conservative mode throughout the 1970s, 80s and 90s into the new millennium, although boards and canvases were eventually substituted for bark. Later transformations of the style were to occur. This is an example of the creatives having a win with design innovation.

A second example is a painting by another Lardil creative whom I wrote about earlier, Thungalgunyaldin (Jackson Jacob). In 1974, he executed a painting for me after deeply thinking about a question I posed: What did his ancestors think a British sailing ship was in the early 1880s? He rendered the painting on bark with the standard crosshatched background but with an innovative image of the Rainbow Serpent wrapped around the hull of the ship and its three masts depicted as decorated poles of the type used in ceremonies (see Figure 13). Jackson explained that it was Thuwathu stealing the dancing ground of somebody who had committed a law

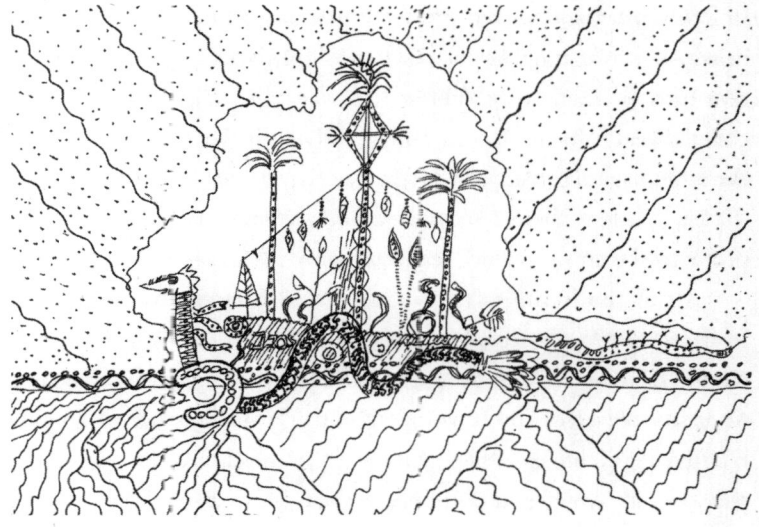

FIGURE 13: Line drawing of a painting by Lardil artist Jackson Jacob, illustrating how he thought his grandfather would have interpreted the first Western sailing ships in the southern Gulf of Carpentaria.

misdemeanour. This was a designer hypothesising and decision-making at his best, but within the framework of traditional law knowledge and in the spirit of a gift to me.

VALUES IN TIN AND BARK

One of my earliest memorable encounters in Aboriginal camps and settlements was with 'tin' – or, more precisely, galvanised iron or 'GI'. The tin town camps that my student colleagues and I first visited in 1972 were in Mount Isa and Cloncurry and north-west Queensland. Then in 1973 I saw more in Normanton and Burketown in the

Gulf Country, and visited the 'tin' mission camp at the Presbyterian mission on Mornington Island. In 1974, I found myself living in a tent next to my new neighbour Runaway Billy Bismark in a camp called 'West End' in Dajarra. Billy, a railway fettler from the Eastern Arrernte, had constructed a modest enclosed cube-shaped tin house for his family with an attached outdoor kitchen, including a hearth protected by an iron windbreak for his wife Maisie.

All of the humpies (self-constructed houses) and structures in these camps displayed interesting design features. With a few simple hand tools, iron sheeting could be readily cut, bent, drilled, folded or recycled, and it was relatively light to transport. I quickly realised that there were lessons to learn in the camps not only about sociospatial layouts and character but also, more precisely, about how people organised their everyday activities and behaviours in their own living environments.

One could be tempted to call each living environment a 'house', but I resisted this because much of the domestic activity was invariably outside, and often more outside than inside – 'inside' meaning in an enclosed shelter with roof and walls; and 'outside' including windbreaks and shade shelters, which were often made of sheets of iron as well, and also one or more hearths, outdoor sleeping places, and food-processing and storage furniture and equipment. Multiple hearths could mean different types of fires for different tasks, or for different gender use, or for different times of the day or night. Sometimes there were water drums and ground roasting pits as well as old cars under repair or stripped for parts. I noticed a recurring property of the living space to be the practice of raking or sweeping, which defined the living area and generated an outer rim or zone of loose debris: this defined a territory of sorts, a privacy threshold at which one had to make a verbal indication to advance in. I started calling this living environment, which was usually a roughly oval or circular shape, the 'domiciliary space'. To call it a 'yard' didn't seem appropriate as there wasn't any formal land tenure for the resident, or rectangular plots or fences. It was all very organic. Figure 14 shows a view of the West End camp when I lived there in 1974.

I also came to understand that the patterns of living I encountered in rural towns were not only culturally specific with recurring properties but also probably derived from the ancient behavioural patterns of the classical or pre-European contact period. They were a product of gradual cultural change over 150 years or so, involving adaptation to increased stationary living and assimilation of second-hand materials such as iron sheeting, wire, fencing posts, canvas, timber and metallic utensils.

FIGURE 14: View of the West End town camp at Dajarra, north-west Queensland, in 1974, showing a bough shed with a bed supported on 5-gallon drums; a shaded shelter for sleeping during the day; a low-roofed structure over a wood stove for wet-weather cooking; and another humpy behind.

By 1975, I was travelling further west into the Northern Territory and seeing a mixture of bush materials and iron in the camps. I realised that to design culturally appropriate houses for Aboriginal clients, these living patterns – both in space and time, and in terms of gendered activities – had to be fully understood. Accelerated and culturally appropriate housing supply for Aboriginal communities had been implemented by the Whitlam government in 1973,[14] but it meant resisting the standard state government practice (as in Queensland) of house design as an instrument for the policy of assimilation. Such a policy assumed that every Aboriginal family would receive the equivalent of a standard worker's cottage and come to live like a white family. Town camps (or fringe camps as they were commonly called then) were places where young architects could learn how Aboriginal people organised and planned their living environments in a way that suited them to achieve their own needs. The only problem was that in the early 1970s, local governments and departments were bulldozing the last fringe camps.

An example from 1975 was a young architect out of Sydney University, Ken George, who was sent with modest federal funding to Wilcannia in western New South Wales, where there were town camps called the Mallee and the Mission. Based on his 1973 study of these camps, he tried to implement a radical self-build project for Barkandji families, taking lessons from the humpy builders' floor plans. He aimed to start a process that shared the budget across all families so that they could all build house modules, adding bedrooms one by one as funding became available and with their own manufactured concrete blocks, all done in a common design pattern adaptable for any size of household. This spatial layout pattern followed the technological design adaptation of humpy extension and expansion. The project met with serious resistance from local government and other tiers of government, and ground to a halt after a few years. Its underpinning Aboriginal design principles were too visionary for the conservative bureaucracies of the era.[15]

Meanwhile, my UQ colleague Peter Bycroft and I had gone to the upper Darling Basin. We arrived by invitation of the Bohda Housing Co-operative at Goodooga on the Bokhara River, where there was an extensive town camp and where we met the chairman, Ernie Skuthorpe. This camp was an Aboriginal reserve that had been excised from the town common many decades previously. We went on to Brewarrina and noted in the tin camps unique styles of shade structures with flat-roofed tops and west-facing skillions.

Recalling this experience some three decades later, I sent a student from UQ, Stephanie Smith, to meet the community to see if they were interested in her providing some sort of research service. She met Clem Orcher and his wife, Isabel, and formed an immediate rapport. She learnt from others that Clem was a renowned master builder of humpies in the Darling Basin, being contracted by Aboriginal clients on other reserves to design and build comfortable humpy houses for them. Clem was able to provide innovative, low-cost solutions with a concrete slab, carpet, curtains, and air-conditioning powered by a generator at a tenth the cost of a conventional government house. Official building approval was somehow avoided for temporary dwellings and there was no rent on Aboriginal land, which appealed to those who subscribed to sovereignty!

Stephanie learnt of other master humpy builders in the Darling Basin, too. Their work could be recognised particularly through signature construction details (a form of personal referencing) that represented their creative contributions to this genre of 'The Tin Camp', as Stephanie later titled her research thesis. Such details included window installation, door hinging and securing design, and jointing techniques of major structural components.

Another exciting outcome of Stephanie's work was that she found the Skuthorpe family and did a measured drawing of their domestic complex, which had expanded and evolved through many tin modules to result in a most complex organic plan (see Figure 15). It resonated with Peter Hamilton's findings in the Mimili pastoral camp of the spinifex dome structures (see Chapter 4), having a similar outward character;

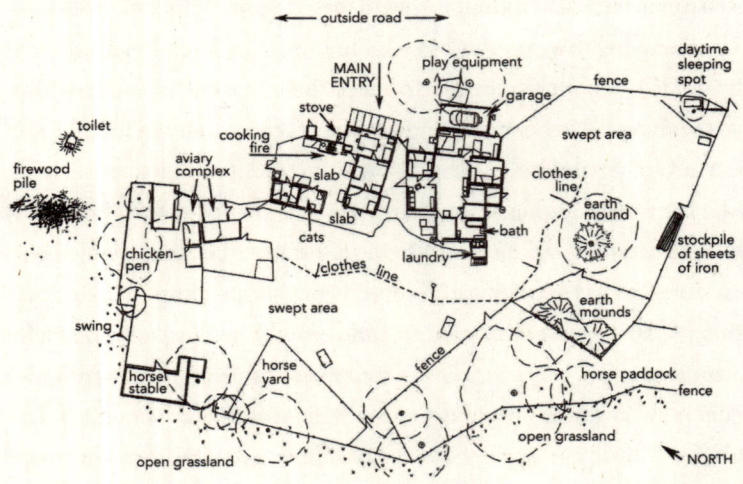

FIGURE 15: Floor plan of the late Ernie Skuthorpe's self-constructed residence, Goodooga, 1992.[16] (It does not look like a suburban house!)

but upon internal inspection of the timber-limb framing structures, discernible signature styles (stylistic techniques) were evident.

If these camps exploited the versatile properties of galvanised iron, what was the equivalent in the classical pre-contact camps? The answer, of course, is sheets of bark – flat, relatively stiff eucalyptus bark and soft, pliable melaleuca paperbark (see Chapter 3). Some occupants decorated the internal walls of their more permanent shelters with painted designs or feather collages. And, of course, the tradition of bark painting evolved into contemporary international high art of great commercial and aesthetic value.

Bark sheets had many design functions, from bedding and food serving to wrapping food to be put in an oven (see Figure 16), wrapping treasured objects and bandaging flesh wounds, to making water carriers and dancing hats, to the more sophisticated bark canoe designs whose joints were carefully sewn and caulked with resin.[17] A most outstanding engineered example was the unique cylindrical fish trap built in the Glyde River vicinity of Arnhem Land (see Figure 17).[18]

One of my PhD students, Cathy Keys, who lived at Yuendumu in the central west Northern Territory in the late 1990s and worked with elders of the Warlpiri single women's camps, or *jilimi*,[19] has written an excellent paper with historian Ray Kerkhove on the widespread significance of Aboriginal bark technology for the first generations of colonial settlers from Britain.[20] The first houses for many of these Anglo-Celtic colonists were simple timber-framed gable cottages with walls and roofs of bark sheeting. Of course, the worst of these settlers stole the bark out of Aboriginal camps, taking it by force.

FIGURE 16: Ground ovens used by the Lardil people of Mornington Island for cooking different types of food.

But increasingly, when the value of their skills was recognised, local Aboriginal people were employed to obtain, process, supply and often install the bark sheeting. A technological knowledge of the available bark species and their relative weatherproofing and manufacturing properties was a prerequisite. The bark contractors also had to know the appropriate time of the year according to rainfall patterns as to when the bark of each species lifted off the trunk slightly and hence could be levered off. How to detail the fixing of the 1 metre × 2 metre sheets of bark to the frame using various sorts of Aboriginal-manufactured string or rope ties, such that they would not split or

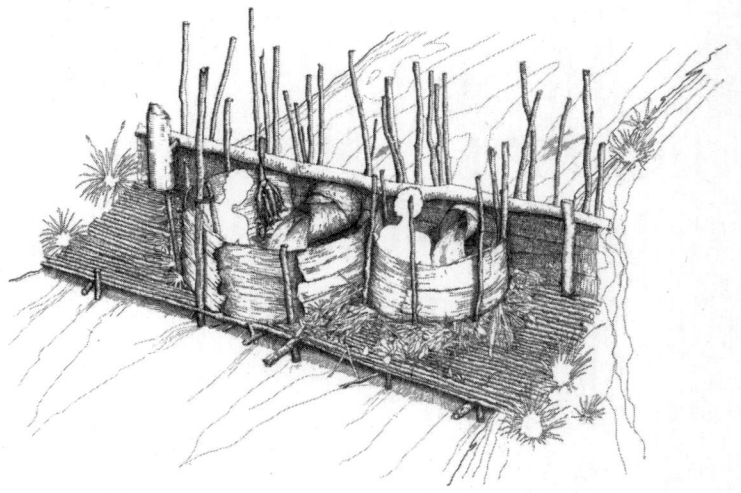

FIGURE 17: Yolŋu men sitting inside two cylindrical fish traps, Glyde River, Arnhem Land.

pull away causing leaks, was another design skill. A valuable cross-cultural transfer of technology occurred to provide frontier housing for the colonial settlers, a humane service that has been historically forgotten or overlooked.

Of course, there is another aspect of traditional Aboriginal design that was not so readily visible to the outside observer of the old societies in Australia: the social principles in designing and controlling the layouts of Aboriginal camps or settlements.

6

CAMP LAYOUTS AND THE IMPORTANCE OF KINSHIP

MY FIRST EXPERIENCE OF AN ABORIGINAL CAMP

PAUL MEMMOTT

My first trip to north-west Queensland was when I was a 22-year-old architecture student, as a member of a group sent by Canberra bureaucrat Nugget Coombs in 1972 to investigate applications from local people for new building projects for the Aboriginal community. It was at the start of shifts in government policies towards self-determination, and the era under the Whitlam government that aimed to house all Aboriginal people in Australia in conventional houses. The trip to Dajarra and to its 'West End' town camp was my first close encounter with humpies. In Mount Isa, the regional centre of north-west Queensland, we encountered the Yallambie Camp (Black Cockatoo Dreaming place), a large complex of self-constructed humpies arranged in clusters in a semi-sedentary camp; this brought my first understanding of an Aboriginal sociospatial camp layout. It was the beginning of my investigation of the continent-wide design of camps, and what I term the 'sociospatial patterns' of Australian Aboriginal settlements, whereby camp layouts are organised in clusters of shelters involving some principle of common social identity or relationship between the people in each cluster or spatial unit (see Figure 18).

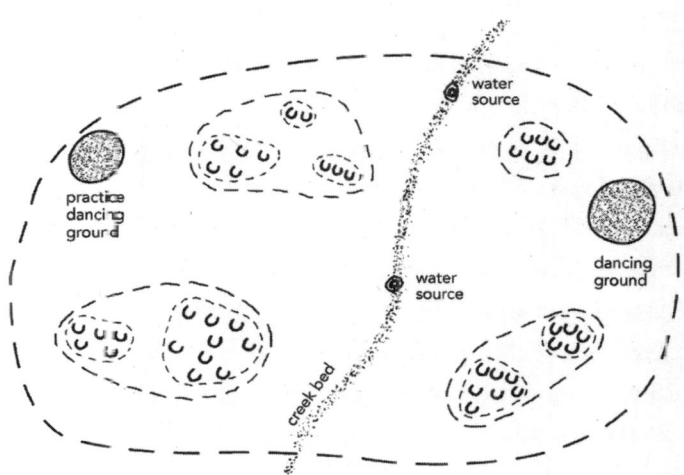

FIGURE 18: An example of a sociospatial pattern in a medium-sized camp, showing four clusters each containing subclusters of shelters (nested clustering). The people in each individual cluster and subcluster would share some common social relation or identity.

SOCIAL AND SPATIAL DESIGN OF LARGE CAMPS

Traditional Aboriginal camps were complex units of place whose size and duration of occupation varied. They ranged from small camps occupied by one or several domiciliary groups for a few days (each being either a family, some single men or single women), to large camps of a specialised nature containing several or more local groups for up to six weeks (or more when food supplies were plentiful). Seasonally available foods, together with prevailing climatic conditions and local climatic changes, were factors influencing the size and spatial structure of camps, shelter types, hunter-gatherer methods, use of certain artefacts, diet and movement patterns.

In better-watered areas, the seasonal camps were often economically specialised. For example, at Mornington Island in the Gulf of Carpentaria, the Lardil had regular dugong and turtle feasting camps; camps from which to exploit particular runs or schools of fish and crops of fruits or vegetables (waterlily camps, pandanus camps and so on); and camps from which to collect specific materials for artefact manufacture. Most Australian coastal groups enjoyed camps of this type. For desert and semidesert dwellers, the larger perennial water sources (particularly waterholes) were important considerations for where a group might camp. As we saw in the case of Lake Francis on the Georgina River (Chapter 4), waterholes provided venues for large-scale social and ceremonial gatherings because they were able to sustain groups for some months with the local plant and aquatic foods and the animals that came to drink the water. They were also vital refuges during sustained periods of drought. On this phenomenon in Central Australia, based on his time living with the Warlpiri some seventy years ago, the anthropologist Mervyn Meggitt wrote:

> Comparatively large groups of perhaps 400 to 500 Walbiri assembled on these [ceremonial] occasions. I may point out here that gatherings of this size were more common in the desert than is generally realized. Thus ... in some localities parties of several hundred Aranda and Matuntara congregated for four or five months at a time. Similarly ... groups of up to 300 Pintupi were observed in the arid South-west Aboriginal Reserve as recently as 1925.[1]

Such large camps have been reported in many other parts of Aboriginal Australia.[2] Although it was the environmental factors that enabled the formation of these camps, other social, religious and economic factors also motivated people to assemble there.

In large camps, social interaction was intensified. News and gossip were exchanged; recent deaths, births and disputes reviewed (significantly, this tradition continues today, either informally at regular outdoor urban meeting places, or during Indigenous political marches and rallies, sporting carnivals and annual celebration days such as NAIDOC). The camp acted as a centre for information dissemination. Individuals continually attended to their position in the social structure so as to facilitate proper kinship behaviour with others. Jealousies, disputes and fights were likely among rivals for potential marriage partners. There were also many customary forms of spatial behaviour. The location and orientation of one's sitting position were chosen carefully to enable ease of communication with appropriate categories of relatives. When approaching or passing close to domestic spaces, auditory signals were purposely used to make others aware of one's presence. At night, one could hear singing, mourning, quarrels and discussion of tomorrow's plans.

Aboriginal residential groups imposed upon themselves a spatial definition in accompaniment to their social identity when forming large-scale camps. This was amply reported by ethnographers of the 19th and early 20th centuries.[3]

DESIGNING SOCIAL PATTERNS INTO THE LAYOUTS OF CAMPS

There are two distinct types of behavioural patterns that may influence the layout of camps, or what I call 'sociospatial structures'. One involves the arrival of a large group at an already-occupied camp site, and the hosts then strategically allocating sites on which the visiting subgroups can establish their shelters, thereby generating spatial divisions according to shared rules. The other involves 'social accretion', whereby an individual or a domiciliary group arrives at an existing camp and attaches themselves to another group on the basis of an existing social link. Such an attachment may set off relocations of other domiciliary groups in the camp, due particularly to avoidance rules (the need for certain members of the group to remain apart socially and spatially, and to avoid eye contact) or perhaps economic ties, until a satisfactory arrangement results. At a certain threshold of size and complexity of relationships, subcamp formation occurs; and eventually, in some cases, subcamp-cluster formation and the even finer-grained subdivisions of nested clustering.

In many cases, the pattern generation in camps involved a composite of both processes. Sociospatial transformation also occurred on a daily basis, as the more tightly structured night-time groupings gave way in the morning to groups for the day's activities, and vice versa in the evening. Men and women would leave their family sleeping groups in the morning and form separate women's food-gathering and men's hunting groups or, alternatively, separate ritual groups.

In designing the social patterning of their camp layouts, traditional Aboriginal societies employed a range of principles of social organisation. The most commonly used principles drew from kinship, social class systems and local groups. These were all very complex systems with much variation across the continent.

Kinship

Kinship was an all-pervasive medium in Aboriginal camps, generating both links and distancing between particular domiciliary groups (whether families, single men or single women). There were rules for the sharing of, and access to, food and other material items and resources. For example, in some groups a woman had to provide food and water for her mother's brother, and a man may ask his brother's wife for food or to obtain a drink.[4] Some of the rules and obligations based on kinship affected everyday behaviours for particular groups, such as which way one should face in a small-group setting, if and when one must leave a group upon the arrival of another person, and the necessity to sometimes pass information to another through a third person. In other cases, circumspect behaviour arose from respect between two individuals who had junior and senior status respectively in a common secret totemic group.

The founder of modern Australian anthropology, Adolphus Elkin, argued that the principles underlying the various rules, avoidances and taboos were broadly the same throughout Australia:

> the [behavioural] avoidances are not expressions or signs of hostility; they are associated with the making of gifts and the performance of duties, often mutual; indeed, betrothals and marriages from which some of the avoidances arise are themselves acts of reciprocal exchange which serve to bind individuals and groups together.[5]

Avoidance between a male and his mother-in-law was a widespread kinship requirement that shaped sociospatial structure. An incoming man and his family would position themselves in the camp at a suitable distance from his mother-in-law's shelter to satisfy their avoidance protocol.

Domestic clustering based on father–child relationships was also prevalent in many groups. The Nunggubuyu of eastern Arnhem Land, for example, had a three-level patrilineal-type sociospatial structure, arranged as nested clusters.[6] It started with a division of the camp site into clusters, each containing a different patriclan – that is, a group whose membership is determined on the basis of patrilineal (father–child) descent from a common ancestor.[7] These clans might have further internal clustering based on separation of the lineages of the most senior brothers. The final camping unit was that of each nuclear family: a man with his wife (or wives) and their children.

In very large camps, patriclan camping areas might be organised according to larger-scale geographic groups. This nested clustering of groups thus imposes a more complex picture on settlement sociospatial structures. Even if everyone in the camp can speak the same language, there may still be divisions based on geographic groupings that are larger than individual patriclans. An example of this was an intertribal trading camp on a channel crossing at Gununa (maximum population 400) at Mornington Island around 1914. It was divided into four subcamps based on geographic units (north, east, south, west) at an intermediate level of structure between language group and patriclans. This generated three tiers of grouping: first, four separate spatial zones in which each of the geographic divisions camped; second, the division of each geographic group into separate patriclan areas; and third, separation into family groups, each with its own shelter and fire.

As a universal principle for Aboriginal Australia, however, camping next to the people of one's neighbouring clans is clearly at odds with camp layouts based on class or skin divisions.

Social class or skin divisions

Kinship links were (and still are for many groups) extendable from local groups to a much broader population, due to the overlaying of class or division systems that allow the classification of even distant strangers as kin. Of complex design, these social class systems involve categories such as moieties (two broad intermarrying classes), sections (four classes or skin groups) and subsections (eight classes or 'skins'). They are still observed in the more remote parts of Australia and by some individuals in eastern rural and metropolitan settings. Kinship relations are assigned to members of the various classes despite the fact that people may not be related by blood or marriage. All people in a society and within a region will be related in a classificatory[8] sense through the use of such a subsystem. Figure 19 shows an Arrernte subsection system from Central Australia involving eight skins. The systems are used to classify not only people but also sacred sites, natural species, objects and songs.[9]

Social class or 'skin' subsystems of social organisation could play a dominant role in the layout of camps, especially in Central Australia. The most outstanding known and mapped example of nested clustering is the Arrernte camp reported by ethnographers Baldwin Spencer and Frank Gillen in 1896, based on eight subsection classes (see Figure 19). Here, there was a primary spatial division within the night-time camp into skin pairs (father–child pairs of skins), and then a breakdown into the men of one subsection or skin and their families.

In this example, single-gender daytime camps also formed, based on skin-pair links and consisting of both classificatory father–son pairs and classificatory aunty–niece pairs (a woman and her brother's daughter). There were also numerous avoidance rules for various categories of relatives, ranging from the broad (skin-pair groups) to the narrow (mother-in-law avoidance).

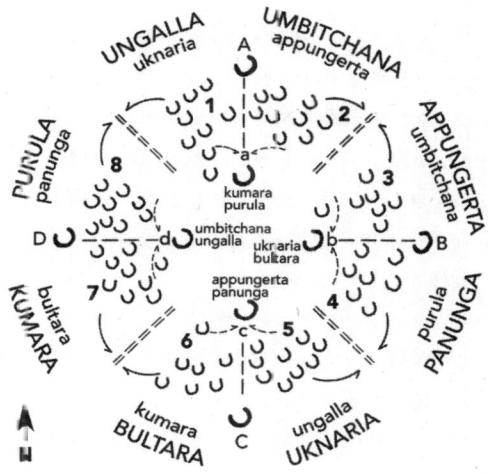

FIGURE 19: Sociospatial structure of a large Arrernte camp gathered for a ceremonial festival in 1896 near Alice Springs Telegraph Station, Northern Territory, illustrating subcamp clustering according to class identity.[10]

1 to 8: Eight subsection groups of the Arrernte. The three-quarter circles indicate night-time windbreaks, which were largely occupied by nuclear families. In each subsection group, the male spouses of each nuclear family share the same social class, which is indicated in upper case (e.g. 'KUMARA'). Accompanying the class name of each male domestic head is that of his wife, in lower case (e.g. 'bultara').

Pairs of subsection groups form subcamp clusters whose male domestic heads comprise a skin pair (father–son category). For example, the KUMARA and PURULA men and their spouses and children form a subcamp cluster; KUMARA and PURULA form a skin pair.

A, B, C and D: Four daytime meeting shelters of the men, called *arnkwentye*, each containing the men from two specific subsections, or a skin pair, plus visitors.

━━━▲ Directions in which the men from each class must walk when circling the camp to visit another group's arnkwentye.

a, b, c and d: Four daytime meeting shelters of the women, called *arlwekere*, each containing the women from two specific subsections, or a skin pair, plus visitors.

━ ━ ━▲ Directions in which the women from each class must walk when circling the camp to visit another group's arlwekere.

115

Another type of class system prevalent in the Western Desert is 'generation moieties', in which a person is categorised with both their real and classificatory siblings, cousins, grandparents and grandchildren while separated from both their real and classificatory parents, uncles, aunts, children, great-grandparents and great-grandchildren – that is, six generations are divided alternately into two categories.[11]

A less common type of moiety division was employed in the Darling River region of western New South Wales for daytime camps: that of 'blood moieties', a subsystem involving unusual symbolic categories – associations of human blood types, tree sap types, tree sap viscosity, tree shade areas and particular sitting positions in such shade for groups having the different blood types.[12]

The locational principle

Each local group has an attachment to a defined piece of Country. This system of social organisation comprises another important form of grouping that was (and is) manifested in the design of many camp layouts. The widespread locational principle prescribes that people coming together in any large camp for economic or ceremonial purposes will take up their positions in clusters according to the direction they came from – north, south, east or west, as if set by a compass.

However, researchers do not agree about the precise reason for this prescription. Many talk of camping in the direction of homeland as a consequence simply of the direction of approach of groups coming into a large camp. Another common cause proposed for this phenomenon is ease of retreat in the case of conflicts arising in the camp. However, an alternative hypothesis, probably more plausible, is that there are culturally distinct notions of respect and privacy associated with approach behaviour and campsite selection behaviour. Some researchers speak of subcamp groups replicating sociogeographic patterns, as if there is a conscious attempt to generate a sociospatial structure signifying a map of the land tenure of local groups.

FUNCTIONS OF SOCIOSPATIAL DESIGN

A range of functional explanations can be put forward to explain Indigenous sociospatial design in Australian camps: expressing and maintaining kin relationships through behavioural style; expressing and reinforcing social group identities of various forms; an expression of the economic dependency among and within domiciliary groups; achieving a certain style of group privacy in camps; minimising conflict among groups through distancing and concepts of 'respect'; and safety of retreat to homeland. These considerations do not all operate at once, although several of them may be prevalent in a particular camp.

It is difficult to identify a single common social function of clustering. In cases where the sociospatial units in camps corresponded closely to the sociogeographic ones on Country, it could be argued that the camp units were a behavioural manifestation of the Country units, derived from the traditional hunter-gatherer lifestyle. That is, the smaller 'building blocks' of camps comprised families who traditionally associated for most of the seasonal year for hunting or fishing (for example, a patriclan with relationships through father–child links), while the members of each larger-scale sociospatial unit (a sociogeographic division, or a dialect group), although associating at times for economic or ritual purposes, would do so less frequently throughout the year than the former, but more frequently than those groups collectively comprising the largest camps. Familiarity and ease with residential neighbours would be the underlying basis of the sociospatial ties and tiers in the larger camps. An early pioneer anthropologist, Ursula McConnel, wrote of western Cape York Peninsula:

> Throughout the camp there extends from one camp fire to another a chain of kinship, more intimate between some families than others, closer between some clans than others, and between some tribes than others. This relative intimacy largely corresponds to the local proximity of intermarrying clans and tribes on their own grounds.[13]

It's clear sociospatial systems still run deep in Indigenous communities, but contemporary Australian design and planning has been slow to recognise that.

7

PLACEMAKING IN COUNTRY

LEARNING ABOUT CLASSICAL ABORIGINAL PLACEMAKING

PAUL MEMMOTT

One day in 1974, I was invited on a dinghy trip from the Mornington Island Presbyterian Mission up to Langunganji (Sydney Island) by a group of Larumbenda Lardil dugong hunters. They were mostly younger men in their twenties and thirties but their leader was an elder, old Jarrar (Bluefish, or Fred Jaurth), who was to become a lifelong friend and teacher to me. The group of six carried minimal gear for an overnight camp, whereas I had a big swag and a backpack with food and utensils! I was about to be given an abundance of lessons but was barely aware of the significance of what was happening: I was involved in the establishment of a temporary travellers' camp on what was a major base-camp site of the Lardil in traditional times before the mission was established in 1914. Jarrar was about twenty years old in 1914 and his family did not come into the mission permanently until the mid-1920s, so he had a wonderful knowledge of the Old People's ways.

I had already learnt that the name of the base camp we were to use was Kenthawu. It was situated on Mornington Island, from which we could easily visit the nearby island of Langunganji, about 2 kilometres across a channel. This was to be my first reconnoitre of Langunganji, to which I would return several times.

When we reached the site of our base camp, Fred barked directives. Two of the younger men, Gordon Watt and Horace Hills, walked off along the beach while a third, Teddy Moon, walked into the open bloodwood country behind the wide sand platform, carrying his tomahawk. Old Tom Jacob and Fred headed in the opposite direction up the beach towards a rock platform below the cliffs at Kupare Point, carrying only their three-pronged fishing spears (*kurrumbu*; see Figure 20). I got to work moving our dugong hunting gear and water bottles and my ample swag up the beach.

Before long, Teddy came back with a dozen sapling stakes. He planted them in a circle of about 5 metres diameter and then took me to collect firewood. Gordon and Horace were next to return, with a great mass of a beach vine known as *thaburru* (*Cassytha filiformis*) that they separated and draped over the stakes to make a 1-metre-high

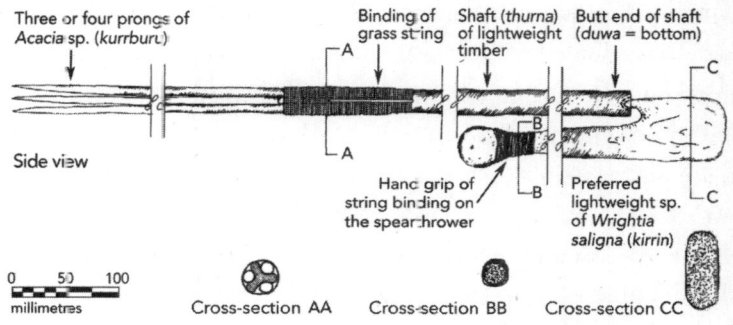

Three or four prongs of
Acacia sp. (kurrburu)

Binding of
grass string

Shaft (thurna)
of lightweight
timber

Butt end of shaft
(duwa = bottom)

Side view

Hand grip of
string binding on
the spearthrower

Preferred
lightweight sp.
of Wrightia
saligna (kirrin)

0   50   100
millimetres

Cross-section AA

Cross-section BB

Cross-section CC

FIGURE 20: Detailed side view and cross-sections of the Lardil fishing spear, *kurrumėu*, and the spearthrower, *murruku*.

FIGURE 21: Constructing the windbreak at Kenthawu on Mornington Island in 1974. The sacred site of Kupare Point is in the left background, with the low-lying Langunganji (Sydney Island) behind.

windbreak (*wungkurr*, see Figure 21). As they were finishing, Fred and Tom returned with a bucket of mud crabs and several large fish they had speared. The crabs had been skilfully extracted from cavities in the rock platform by spear or by hand.

Soon we were sitting at dusk in the glow of the warm camp fire with fish and crabs roasting in the ashes and coals, each with a bundle of oak-tree branches on which to serve our feast. Fred began 'telling the Country' – the sacred histories of the *Mirndiyan* (Dreaming) in the vicinity – but I was too young and white (colonised!) to fully understand the significance, unaware that the spirits of the ancestors were watching over us. Nevertheless, I was in the safety of a Lardil hunters' overnight travelling camp, with its comforts being used in the way they had been for centuries, and benefiting from the 'kindness of Country' as many generations had before.

The following winter I returned to Mornington Island and Langunganji to begin an eight-month field trip. One of my major tasks was to fully map the Lardil geography, camp sites, seasonal resources and story places (sacred sites) of two clan countries: that of old Fred of the Larumbenda division, and that of old Kelly Bunbujee of the Lilumbenda (eastern) division. These two elders had lived a fully traditional lifestyle in their youth before the Presbyterian mission was established and stabilised after the spearing of the first missionary – a time they could clearly describe. I did not know at the time that I was to be one of the last anthropological researchers to work with such wise Old People.

Our 1974 camp was a striking example of a travellers' camp: a culturally constructed domestic setting that employs minimal (if any) structure.[1] A travellers' camp is quickly made and comprises domestic spaces, a hearth and artefacts, and sometimes a windbreak or shade; it is used overnight or perhaps for only a few hours (such as for 'dinner' or a midday camp) by a group travelling through Country. As there is little time to spend constructing a shelter, the natural qualities of the chosen site are very important for enhancing residential comfort. Although travellers' camps continue to be in daily use in many remote parts of Australia, not many examples have been officially recorded.

AN ALYAWARR TRAVELLERS' CAMP

Let us wind forward some ten to fifteen years to the Sandover River in the Wakaya Desert of Central Australia, to another of my teachers, old Paddy Woodman – a revered elder of the Alyawarr nation or language group – and a younger man, Steven Bob (Paddy's nephew). Paddy's 'skin' was *kemarre*, like mine, so I was privileged to call him older brother, whereas he addressed me as younger brother. It was while travelling with Paddy, who at this time was about eighty-five years old, that I clearly came to understand the design ingredients of classic Aboriginal place through the lens of the travellers' camp.

Paddy's preferred campsite location was mulga woodland. He would be grumpy if there were no mulga-tree communities available on the late-afternoon route at which to camp for the night. In other types of tree communities, there are more likely to be prickles, burrs, grass and ground cover that can shelter snakes, centipedes, scorpions or nests of stinging ants; the floor of a mulga forest is free of grass and easy to sweep clean of loose dirt and needle leaves with a branch. Mulga is also a superior wood for cooking and warming fires as it produces long-burning, ash-free hot coals. In the mulga camp one notices the whirl of certain fast-flying flocks of birds that adopt the mulga as their habitat. There is also a constant familiar and secure sound of wind in mulga.[2]

Yarning at night around the camp fire with Paddy ranged across many topics but included reflection on the Aboriginal history of the region surrounding the camp site – for example, the totemic history and creation of sacred sites by Ancestral Beings, the history of mortals from past generations in perpetuating the Dreaming history in ceremonial performance and sacred site maintenance, and the violent contact clash with white pastoralists who settled here from the 1890s to the 1930s.

Paddy and Steven slept side by side with a small mulga fire burning between them. Several long mulga limbs protruded to one side of their sleeping area and were gradually fed into the fire through the night. Paddy travelled with a 'swag' of two thin, frayed blankets; at night he spread one under and one over himself. He always slept in his clothes and pointed his head to the east and feet to the west to prevent the infiltration of bad spirits during sleep. In the early morning, his first activity after sitting up was warming and smoking the inside of his hat over the fire. Steven blew and fanned the embers to produce flames for boiling tea.[3]

The properties of this camp illustrate the various elements required for human comfort. A selected site or 'position in the landscape' ensures that there are comforts of surface, vegetation, sound, smell, warmth, security, spatial definition, customary domestic behaviours and connection with the animals and plants in the habitat (see Figure 22). In the circumstance of a strong wind, a windbreak can be quickly constructed of mulga limbs. If there is a shower of rain, the fire can be stoked up. During the early contact period, persistent rain would possibly have resulted in the construction of a foliage-clad dome, but on this trip, we would have stretched a plastic sheet or blanket over a shrub.

This is 'architecture' at its most minimal, but it is not 'primitive', as some might call it, because the campers retain a certain level of comfort and aesthetic. Security stems from the environmental positioning in the mulga grove and the shared understanding of the totemic meanings attached to the cultural landscape in which

FIGURE 22: Aboriginal men Paddy Woodman (right) and Steven Bob from the Alyawarr nation, Central Australia, awakening in their overnight camp while travelling on ceremonial business in the 1980s.

the camp site is located, to which each person has a particular kinship relation (a Python Dreaming man like Paddy, for example, marries a Kangaroo Dreaming woman). The campers are nurtured by, and receive kindness from, the camp site and the cultural landscape, which provides for their human and social needs.

Australian Aboriginal architecture can therefore be defined as architecture that is a selected, arranged and constructed configuration of environmental properties, both natural and artificial, in and around one or more activity spaces, combined with patterns of behavioural rules and meanings, to result in human comfort and quality of lifestyle. This definition includes selected environmental features, mental and behavioural rules, spatial properties, hearths and artefacts. It can also include buildings, but they are not necessary. It incorporates such concepts as sociospatial settlement structure, avoidance behaviour, diversity of construction detailing and its impact on spatial experience, and ceremonial spaces imbued with meaning and theatrical moment. A range of cognitive, invisible, ephemeral and symbolic properties instil Aboriginal architecture with a culturally distinct nature.

Now let us return to Mornington Island and the camp site of Kenthawu.[4]

'HOME' IN LARDIL COUNTRY

At the time of early European contact, the islands of the Lardil people were divided into twenty-nine small countries, or 'estates' (as anthropologists call them), each under the custodianship of a clan and each made up of many individual named places (see Figure 23).

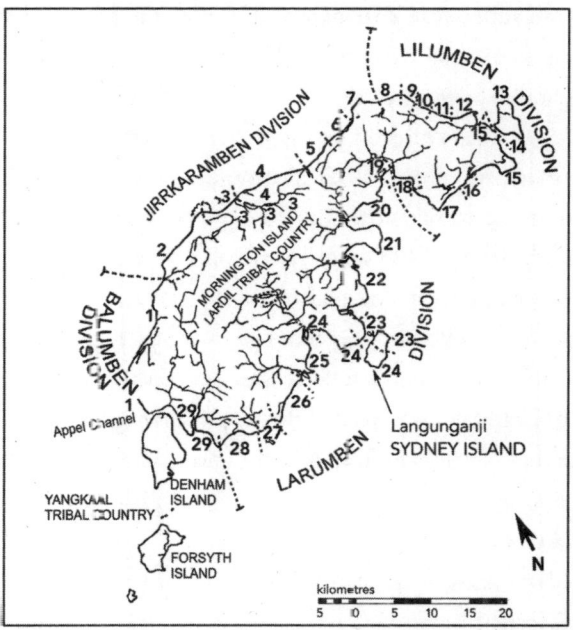

FIGURE 23: Lardil patriclan estates or Countries (numbered), and geographic divisions, Mornington Island, Gulf of Carpentaria, 1975.

Traditional Lardil places (which probably exceeded 1000 in number) were distinguished with individual names, but most did not contain built structures. The older adults knew all of the place names throughout Lardil lands as well as important properties associated with each. They included camp sites, wells, story places, initiation grounds and special resource-collecting places – see, for example, the places on the map of Kenthawu in Figure 24. Lardil elders could also explain the origin of most of the places in their Countries. Generally, they had been created during the travels of Dreaming

Heroes and supernatural beings such as Manhpil, Dewil Dewil and Jin Jin, the creators of coastal landscapes. Thuwathu, the Rainbow Serpent, added power to story places, which enabled 'increase rituals' (actions that were believed to cause a reproduction of the totemic animal, plant or meteorological phenomenon associated with a place) to be performed at them. These places were considered to be the fountainheads of life where particular species could be ritually activated to come forth and multiply.

Dick Roughsey's birthing camp gives another interesting insight into the beliefs and cultural practices related to the idea of being 'homed in Country'. Goobalathaldin, or Dick Roughsey (1920–1985), was a famous Lardil man from Mornington Island who was an artist, a writer and the first chairperson of the Aboriginal Arts Board of the Australia Council. His 1971 book *Moon and Rainbow* was the first published autobiography of an Aboriginal person who lived a classic tribal lifestyle. His father's name was Kiwarbija, meaning 'rolling sea' or 'heavy sea swell', which is how Dick was given the surname Roughsey by the first Presbyterian missionaries on the island. As he explained in *Moon and Rainbow*:

> I was born under a clump of pandanus palms at Gara Gara, just behind Goobirah [Kupare] Point. It must have been somewhere around 1920, but I am not sure of my exact age. When I was about twelve my mother showed me the place where I was born, and said it was at the time of the ripe pandanus nuts, which ripen in September. Naturally my birth name is also Gara Gara [Karrakarra].[5]

Although Dick's Aboriginal name was Goobalathaldin ('rolling sea'), he had a supplementary birthplace name, Karrakarra. In his book he described the story place on nearby Kupare Point and the related sacred history of the native bees that attempted to cross from there to Sydney Island before being chased back by the stingray Balibal, who flapped and splashed droplets of water into the sky to wet the bees' wings if they travelled too far. However, the unedited manuscript contains a much lengthier and richer stream-of-consciousness reflection, and is more useful for understanding the salient properties of this popular camp site in Dick's cultural perception of home Country:

When I was a boy of about 12 my mother showed me the place where I was born, it was a pretty place near a clump of pandanus, at the time of the falling of the ripe pandanus nut about September. The pandanus nuts when green it all stuck together, like and shape as pine-apple when its getting ripe they turned red and when it falls on the ground, and lie there until its dry and browning then its gathered in with bush bark made like basket to carry any food stuff or baby in it ... [After cooking] they then will smack the burnt nut to pieces and careful take out [the kernel] nuts, that taste good. The nut is a small white one and it is milkie when we eat them, it even help mothers in those early days how to keep their breast up with milk for the baby's food.[6]

Here, Dick provides a description of the seasonal times when this camp was utilised and the type of economic activity (pandanus nut harvest) that took place due to the presence of a permanent freshwater well, in conjunction with fishing and dugong hunting. He went on to describe a further specialised function of the camp:

> A birth place was always carefully chosen, plenty of shade from the sun, clean sand, and plenty of firewood to light big fire near mother to keep flies away. The mother was looked after by her sister, or if no sisters another woman of the tribe. My mother was looked after by grandmother Garrandu, wife a member of my father's tribe. And my father stayed away until my skin turned dark … The mother is not allowed to walk over to her father's camp until one month.[7]

As this passage indicates, the resource capacity of the birthing-camp locale was critical for the support of the mother and related midwives for an extended period. Dick described another important seasonal vegetable resource at the camp site:

> Garagara [Karrakarra] is a nice place … Not far away it has a water lily swamp. This water lily is divided to so many people when the lillies are ripe and ready to dig and eat. People are sent as a messenger, to go and bring them all to come from different countries to come and share with the lilly. So then as they are all there … They all divided the part of the swamp to each tribe of people and then we all dig in the swamp and have a good time together.[8]

Memories of the camp site were thus founded on predominantly seasonal occupation characteristics, as well as on special biosocial events such as birthing, feasting and person-naming. Dick also described, for example, the large-scale tribal feasting that would follow a catch of multiple dugong. Figure 24 shows the layout and features of the area.

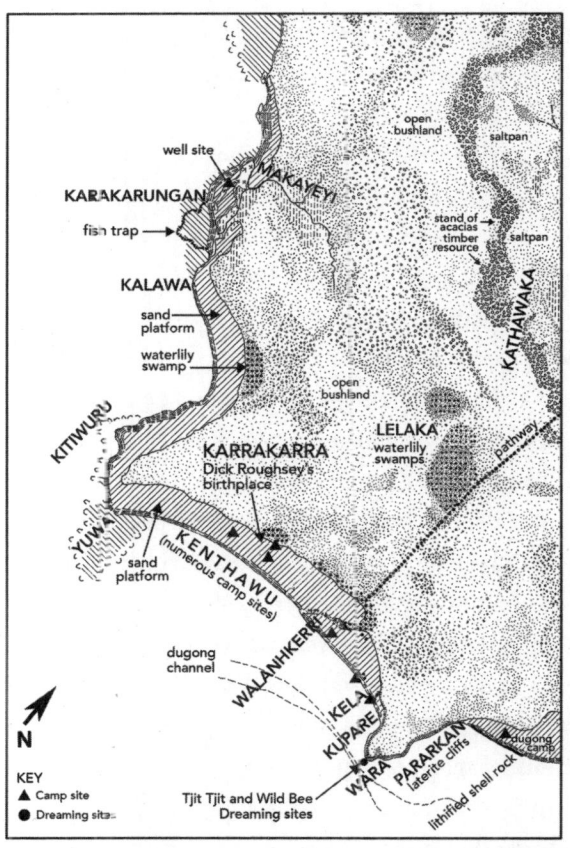

FIGURE 24: Map of Kenthawu beach and sand platform, including Dick Roughsey's birthplace, Karrakarra and Kupare Point.

Lardil camps were complex units of place. They ranged from small camps occupied by one or several domiciliary groups for a few days, to larger camps occupied by three or four domiciliary groups, to even larger ones that could be occupied by several geographic groups (each with twelve or so visiting clans from different Countries) for up to six weeks. Such options for camping were decided within seasonal parameters (the availability of seasonal food harvests, together with the prevailing local climate).

Each Lardil patriclan Country contained multiple camp sites. I mapped nine in Fred's Country and seventeen in the estate of Kelly Bunbujee. At any given time, most Lardil camp sites were unoccupied and, apart from shell middens and old hearths, had few physical structures or markers to indicate their function. Architectural objects did not necessarily contribute to the continuity of a sense of place. However, when the members of a clan arrived at a camp site, they automatically knew what to do in order to make the site functional in a short time – digging out the well, building a shelter, collecting firewood and so on. And because of a consistent pattern of usage, each camp would likely be associated for each adult with a set of previous experiences there. This might include a wealth of memories, daydreams, nostalgia, imagery of people and events, and revelations at sacred sites, extending back in time through the many seasonal movement cycles. Individual shelters were too impermanent to be remembered in this way. 'Home' was thus comprised of the camp sites and other important places in one's Country, but not any particular architectural residence. This is an example of the concept of 'home' being based on Country and sociability rather than a private house as in the contemporary Western world.

Relationships between people, their homeland places and the totemic species of their story places still share special cultural properties that bind all three phenomena together. The Lardil cosmological explanation of these phenomena says that they are interdependent, each providing a consistent set of beliefs for the others. A fourth interdependent domain is that of the Dreaming universe. Links into this world can be found in the landscape, which imbue everyday experience in one's Country as profound, spiritual and personalised. For example, one night when camping at Kenthawu, I was awoken by Fred singing a song in his sleep. He was receiving a gift of knowledge from ancestral spirits about the sacred history of the ancestral warrior Warrenbi and his love for the Wallaby Woman, Maguraa. Individual identity is clearly based on an animal, a plant or some other natural phenomenon, and with that being's story place. Cosmologic and religious thought permeates the nature of Lardil places.

This Aboriginal sense of Country as home was shared by all politically stable Aboriginal groups. The eminent mid-20th century anthropologist William Stanner commented further on the numerous meanings of the classical Aboriginal construct of 'home':

No English words are good enough to give a sense of the links between an Aboriginal group and its homeland. Our word 'home', warm and suggestive though it be, does not match the Aboriginal word that may mean 'camp', 'heart', 'country', 'everlasting home', 'totem place', 'life source', 'spirit centre', and much else all in one. Our word 'land' is too spare and meagre ... The Aboriginal would speak of 'earth' and use the word in a richly symbolic way to mean his 'shoulder' or his 'side'. To put our words 'home' and 'land' together into 'homeland' is a little better but not much. A different tradition leaves us tongueless and earless towards this other world of meaning and significance. When we took what we call 'land' we took what to them meant home, the source and locus of life, and everlastingness of spirit.[9]

THE 'HOUSEHOLD' IN THE ABORIGINAL MODEL OF HOME

In the traditional Aboriginal context, the occupants of a camp constitute the equivalent of a household. It is made up of members of the Country estate or clan and their spouses, and visitors. These are the people, for example, who came together at Dick Roughsey's birthplace camp for seasonal harvests and feasting. However, the social make-up of the residential group is always subject to change due to a complex range of socioeconomic events in the wider region.

Kinship is a driving force behind a household group's social organisation, with its extensive networks of relationships derived from the complex marriage rules about who is eligible to marry whom, and the classificatory kinship naming systems, referred to as skins. The field of relations would also extend to entities beyond the human, such as sacred sites and totemic beings.[10] Just as the idea of 'household' was different in Aboriginal society from the way we think of it in Anglo-Australian society, so were the concepts of 'house', 'home' and 'house design' (see Table 1).

TABLE 1: Summary comparison of the Anglo-Australian and traditional Aboriginal concepts relating to 'house', 'home', 'household' and 'house design'.

ANGLO-AUSTRALIAN CONCEPTS	TRADITIONAL ABORIGINAL CONCEPTS
House (a building)	Domiciliary space with hearth and artefacts (may or may not have a shelter depending on season and weather)
Home (one's regularly used house)	Estate or Country (contains multiple camp sites, resource places and sacred sites)
Household (those living in a home)	Band (patriclan plus spouses and visitors), all maintaining a strong sense of relational personhood
House design (an architectural notion)	Campsite selection, with targeted resource-harvesting strategy and band-group invitations to visit and dwell together (messengers sent), as well as camp layout design according to social and spatial principles

INDIGENOUS PLACEMAKING IN THE CONTEMPORARY WORLD

ALISON PAGE

American urbanist, journalist and organisational analyst William H Whyte is considered the godfather of contemporary placemaking. Since he walked around New York City in the 1970s and carefully observed human behaviour in corporate plazas, urban streets, and parks and other open spaces, 'placemaking' as a design movement has transformed the creation of urban spaces. Through his famous Street Life Project, he studied human interactions, the effect of trees, wind and light, sun and shade, and the gathering of people for cultural activities and food, and found that the physical environments that were being built had little regard for the people who used them. He wrote: 'If there's a lesson in streetwatching it is that people do like basics – and as environments go, a street that is open to the sky and filled with people and life is a splendid place to be.'[11]

The Project for Public Spaces, which was built on Whyte's philosophy, says 'placemaking pays close attention to the myriad ways in which the physical, social, ecological, cultural, and even spiritual qualities of a place are intimately intertwined'.[12] What Whyte was promoting was a return to fundamental principles. He recognised that along the path of modern human evolution we have disconnected from these basic universal human needs. Through the practice of contemporary design, planners of urban spaces have been trying to reconcile high-density built environments with (what seems to me) a primordial experience of human interaction with one another and with nature. Placemaking is a purposeful attempt to pull our primal human instincts into the design of our cities.

Earlier in this chapter, Paul wrote that Australian Aboriginal architecture is 'a selected, arranged and constructed configuration of environmental properties, both natural and artificial, in and around one or more activity spaces, combined with patterns of behavioural rules and meanings, to result in human comfort and quality of lifestyle'. I would like to examine the similarities of these philosophies to find an Indigenous approach to contemporary 'placemaking' in urban design.

As Paul says, the travellers' camp was chosen for 'comforts of surface, vegetation, sound, smell, warmth, security, spatial definition, customary domestic behaviours and connection with the animals and plants in the habitat'. This could easily be a list of prerequisites for any great place, and although urban spaces are generally pre-prescribed locations and so are often retrofitting these desires, the improvement of such spaces can aim to achieve the qualities of a travellers' camp.

Paul also emphasised that the environmental design principles in the camp 'were decided within seasonal parameters (the availability of seasonal food harvests, together with the prevailing local climate)'. As part of good placemaking, the urban designer does consider climatic conditions, but within the limitations of fixed architectural features. The designer often incorporates flexibility within the seasonal year as opposed to adjusting for major shifts in climatic conditions spanning longer periods. At a smaller scale, it seems possible to incorporate more temporary windbreaks and flexible shade structures to respond to the changes in weather on a given day. This as part of the design brief could be expanded, particularly in the Australian context and architectural response to climate change.

But flexibility doesn't just apply to environmental responses: it also relates to the creation of a multitude of social interactions. British human geographer Tim Cresswell describes urban spaces as defined by repeated social practices:

> Place provides the conditions of possibility for creative social practice. Place in this sense becomes an event rather than a secure ontological place rooted in notions of the authentic. Place as an event is marked by openness and change rather than boundedness and permanence.[13]

This resonates with Paul's description of Uncle Jarrar's camp at Kenthawu on Mornington Island, which was set up based on its functional and environmental offerings as well as its location, or what Paul describes as 'positioning in the cultural landscape'.

While the temporary windbreak was being set up, Uncle Jarrar was hunting for a feed. Food is an essential ingredient in the activation and creation of both Western and Indigenous notions of place. The difference between them lies in the fact that the hunting and foraging of food at the locale is a critical part of the Indigenous relationship to place, especially in how that changes seasonally. This is also an interesting brief for inclusion in the design of future cities. What if a place offered people the opportunity to at least forage for seasonally available produce on the site, even if it was a reduced experience? Restaurants might have adjacent gardens where herbs and vegetables can be picked upon ordering, or landscaping may include seasonal agricultural plants such as native grasses to grow what the land wants to grow, or seasonal gardens may be planted that are themed around food and medicine. 'Hunting' for food in the context of city planning could be applied to the tracking and discovery of traditional knowledge at a site. For children, this could be a joyous experience that is integrated into active play areas. It emphasises the essential ingredients of the travellers' camp and is multisensory, with sound, smell and spatial definition as core principles.

In 2019, Indigenous design firm Yerrabingin created a farm on the roof of a multistorey building in Redfern, Sydney. The operators expose visitors to traditional knowledge and sustainable food production by growing a vast array of native bush tucker and giving talks, workshops and educational tours. One of the founders, Christian Hampson, says,

> Our culture is embedded in the landscape and environmental consciousness. Sharing this tacit knowledge and wisdom through a cultural landscape, at this point in time, when our earth is under threat, must be a principle for future landscape design approaches.[14]

This prototype is scalable and replicable not just across Sydney rooftops but in towns and cities all over Australia. Whether a site includes the growing of food or not, breaking bread together is an essential part of the human experience and universally understood as an excellent lubricant for conversation. This is as true now as it has been for millennia. Whyte presented a connection between the lively social vibrancy of the plaza and the presence of food sharing, stating that 'Food attracts people, who attract more people.'[15]

The kind of conversation Paul describes in the travellers' camp with Uncle Paddy reveals the foundation of maintaining one's place in the cultural landscape: 'Yarning at night around the camp fire with Paddy ranged across many topics but included reflection on the Aboriginal history of the region surrounding the camp site – for example, the totemic history and creation of sacred sites by Ancestral Beings [and] the history of mortals from past generations in perpetuating the Dreaming history in ceremonial performance.' This daily ritual strengthens connection to the Dreaming and incorporates modern history, including violent clashes with white pastoralists. It is a deep form of socialisation as it spans generations, and it makes Indigenous ways of knowing unique.

In Whyte's view, a successful plaza for socialisation includes wide steps where people can gather in groups and have conversations in casual arrangements. In the Indigenous way, the interactions between people seem casual but on closer inspection are more formalised and very purposeful. Conversations are centred on strengthening the memory and story of a place and 'placing' the people within the context of that much larger story. One of the foundations of Indigenous placemaking is 'placing people' and their present experience into a narrative that spans 65,000 years. In the design of Indigenous spaces, it is critical that the triggers or mnemonics of the story are integrated into the physical environment to help guide the deep conversations. This is essentially how Songlines can be literally built into the environments we use every day.

'Placing' people in the cultural landscape also includes, as Paul explains in Chapter 6, the 'locational principle' – that is, positioning of people in camps to maintain respect and privacy. In some cases this looks like a map, as people are situated according to the direction they came from. It also has a spiritual dimension. As Paul describes, Uncle Paddy 'always slept in his clothes and pointed his head to the east and feet to the west to prevent the infiltration of bad spirits during sleep'. I find the locational principle a very interesting proposition to build into urban spaces. Imagine plazas being arranged so that people could orientate themselves towards their homelands.

In 2002, I worked at the Adelaide Festival to create an event that involved the locational principle – but before I write about that, I first need to explain the planning of Adelaide. The city was laid out by Colonel William Light, and his plan of 1837 is widely acknowledged as an early example of enlightened city planning. He laid out a distinctive grid pattern of streets and squares based on the square mile, with Victoria Square (Tarntanyangga) in the centre and North, East, South and West terraces as its borders. Hindmarsh (Mukata), Light, Hurtle and Whitmore squares, in the centres of each of the four quadrants of the Adelaide city centre, gave the city a cardinal grid pattern, with King William Street connecting it to the river. When I was consulting with the traditional owners, the Kaurna people, they spoke fondly of Light, saying that he must have consulted with their ancestors in laying out the city.

When you stand in the very centre of Adelaide, in the middle of Victoria Square, you can see the horizon in all four directions. For the festival opening, we planned a dawn ceremony at each of the squares. Audiences were invited to come to the square that corresponded with the direction of their homeland. Then, for the main event in Victoria Square, people entered this modern-day corroboree from that direction also. It was an upscaling of the locational principle and the protocols that surround it in activating the city to become a culturally vibrant place through arts and events.

Some aspects of the traditional cultural landscape are more difficult to translate into urban design, namely the highly organised social and kinship structures of camps described by Paul in Chapter 6. The modern city has different gender associations that form more organically and are not prescribed by lore. Secrecy and ritual, especially in high-density spaces, become a more difficult proposition, although not impossible. As described above, creating new ceremony and ritual as part of an activation program in cities and towns is an unexplored area with high potential for the invigoration of places. I have always thought secrecy could be explored further in terms of interpretive elements in a city. For example, if a trail of traditional knowledge were etched or carved into building surfaces or outdoor furniture or placed in gardens, some of this information could be hidden. When I designed an exhibition for the Powerhouse Museum in 1999 called *Bayagul*, I applied this concept to great effect, hiding objects away in drawers and cupboards so that visitors who rushed through would miss it but those who sat still or moved through multiple times slowly were rewarded. Although it could never equal rites of initiation or lore, it at least paid homage to the notion that information is only passed on to those who have earned it by following the rules and meeting their cultural obligations. There is a lot more to explore in this idea about how we experience knowledge and the mutual obligations required.

Because placemaking is a successful driver for urban design globally, it is worthwhile for Australian cities and towns to overlay the design principles of the travellers' camps studied by Paul: flexibility in architecture, seasonality, food, storytelling, reinforcing the mnemonic of place, integrating traditional knowledge and cultural protocols, and understanding one's position in the cultural landscape. These offer a deeper interpretation of placemaking that expands what Whyte and his contemporaries have built in the vibrant cities of today. It will always start with comforts of surface, vegetation, sound, smell, warmth, security and spatial definition, but ultimately it is about creating a greater connection with nature and each other.

SONGLINES AND THE BUILT ENVIRONMENT

In 2007 my sister, sculptor Tina Lee, and I were commissioned to create a sculpture at the Five Islands Lookout on top of Mount Keira in Wollongong. We were engaged for the project because my colleague Dillon Kombumerri had learnt through initial engagement with the community that it was a women's place: he felt he had no business there. Grateful for the project, Tina and I acted on our instincts and engaged with the local women to co-create the work. As soon as we started learning about the history of the site, an epic creation story emerged of the Five Islands and the mountain, about Oola-boola-woo, the west wind, and his six daughters. That this was the first project I had done on my traditional lands and that Tina and I were from a family of six daughters seemed quite matter-of-fact to the women we were working with, but this massive coincidence was not lost on us. I accepted it and kept unpacking the story, whose meaning, I must admit, has only fully dawned on me lately, because at the time I knew nothing about Songlines.

According to the Dreaming of the Wadi Wadi people, Mount Keira is Geera, one of the daughters of Oola-boola-woo. He and his six daughters, Mimosa, Wilga, Lilli Pilli, Wattle, Clematis and Geera, lived on top of the Illawarra escarpment. When five of the sisters misbehaved, refusing to share with their cousins, Oola-boola-woo punished them by blowing them out to sea, where they turned to stone and became the Five Islands. Geera was left on their escarpment home with no one to play with. She let the plants grow on her and the animals crawl on her until eventually she, too, turned to stone, becoming the mountain who would forever look over her sisters.[16]

Tina and I had many conversations about the story's meaning while we worked, and talked about how this cautionary tale would have been told to countless Wadi Wadi children to ensure they would share, help with chores and be kind to their cousins. I understand the idea of didactic stories and thought at the time that passing on virtues and morals was the primary purpose of our creation stories. What I didn't understand was why the sisters had plant names. The answer lies in the Songlines.

Ancestral Beings from the Dreaming created the land, sky and sea. As they travelled they left Dreaming tracks or Songlines, crisscrossing the country in complex patterns that were laid down and added to over millennia. Passing on complex environmental and cultural data without the written word, the Songlines therefore were what allowed Indigenous people to survive so successfully for so long. Buried inside the Songlines is a massive database of traditional knowledge – a living, ever-evolving storehouse of information about the land, the sea, the sky and the people. It's the library of the Dreaming. And the data that is kept in this library has to make sense because it could be the difference between life and death. The tracks are more than imaginary two-dimensional lines going from A to B. They spiral in every direction, and as you are initiated and passed through ceremony and lore, they become as real as any mountain or river.

Songlines are much more than just wayfinding: they can be visualised as corridors or pathways of knowledge, including knowledge of the stars and seasons, management of the land and sea, and the secret and sacred lore of the land. Every person back in the day knew hundreds, even thousands, of specific facts about their Country and everything in it. It was the people themselves who were the key to activating the library, because as they moved around, engaging in ceremony, they would download and upload knowledge at places of significance. They would share the knowledge with each other and invest it back into the land through, for example, singing the Country, thus keeping the Songlines alive and making the archive a living, breathing database. So everything in the land, sea and sky became the ultimate network for mnemonic learning.

This cultural framework and system of learning was used all over Australia, across hundreds of clans, and is beautifully described by Margo Neale and Lynne Kelly in the first book in this series, *Songlines: The Power and Promise*. Margo writes that Songlines is 'a cross-cultural term for the concept of *Tjukurpa*, *Altyerre*, *Kujika* and other localised terms for Songlines or Dreamings – another introduced and equally well-received Western word. These terms are used interchangeably.'[17]

As an urban Aboriginal woman standing at the Five Islands Lookout and looking out over Wollongong, I am standing on the Dreaming tracks of my ancestors and the sisters of the Five Islands, and their plant names now take on a much deeper meaning. In traditional times the average person knew important facts about hundreds of plants: when they flowered, which parts could be used for potions and which parts were poisonous. Stories about plants personified were able to add more and more layers of data so that the facts eventually became embodied knowledge.

But the story doesn't end there. While this place on the mountain was an important women's place, it was also a place of trauma – a known site of power over life and death. A few weeks before Tina and I started our project, a woman and her nine-year-old son had died there. I still experience this traumatic event viscerally when I go to the site. Ancient and contemporary events continue to inform the identity of this place.

How can all these layers of memory and story be represented? While modern design, architecture and landscape architecture can never replace the oral tradition, they can play a vital role in holding the memories of a site. The memories can be articulated through public art and signage, but can also be communicated as part of the fabric of the architecture, the landscaping and the design of the public realm.

Songlines do not have to incorporate only Indigenous stories. As described in *Songlines*, Lynne's personal attribution of the memory code to her own house, then street, then neighbourhood was a learning journey that any of us can create for ourselves. We can learn Japanese, the countries of Africa or the periodic table by attaching knowledge to places on our daily morning walk. Over time, this information becomes embodied and never leaves us. Just because the particular mnemonic technique explained by Songlines is an Indigenous system of learning doesn't mean that this memory method can't be applied to other content. That is the promise of the *Songlines* book.

In Lynne's research, she worked with traditional owners on Dja Dja Wurrung Country in Victoria and created 'memory trails' in both secondary and primary schools. At Malmsbury Primary School, the students and Lynne assigned historical eras and events to various places on the school grounds – for example, the top of the stairs near the sports area might represent the 1930s and the opening of the Sydney Harbour Bridge; while the school oval might embody the 1960s – an important decade for Aboriginal rights.

Just as Stonehenge in England is emblematic of the site of its creation, it also has a story – an ancestral past associated with the exploits of the creative being(s) who brought these structures into existence. Even stone tools are site specific and have ancestral origins: they have a ceremonial story where associated ancestors and their exploits are celebrated, and a functional story related to their use. Similarly, the symbols and patterns carved into a woomera or a boomerang are often directly related to these story categories – that is, they are formed to make them efficient tools, and they are layered with other ancestral knowledge. We can extrapolate these concepts of the meaning of place embedded in tools to the idea of an institution of learning, such as a school or university. The whole school site, for example, can become an artefact etched with the knowledge of that place that imparts its learning in a way that 'wants you to know'.

The application of these concepts to heritage planning implicates a whole new set of values based on incorporating meanings important to people who are culturally invested in the site as a place of learning and memory. Such an approach resonates with the practice of Indigenous connection to Country. Take an investment of time and history embedded into the three-dimensional world of objects, and multiply it over many generations. The connection to those 'things' and places assumes great depth, and the idea of caring for Country moves to greater levels of clarity and includes the stories and data needed in order to achieve ecological sustainability.

This is why chopping down a tree or blasting through a mountain is akin to walking into a library and setting fire to its books. Denying access to sites is equally devastating, as Margo writes: 'Taking the land was also taking the archive, destroying our identity and raison d'être – not that the colonisers could have conceived of such an alien concept as an archive in the land.'[18] The stories can be modified and added to and certainly the mnemonic can be replaced or renovated, but it is difficult to argue for its wholesale removal. You can't just knock down a tree or remove rocks without replacing them with an equal or better version of the mnemonic or symbol that represents the knowledge in that place.

It is important that the endurance of the narrative outlasts the life cycle of the bricks and mortar. Additional layers can be added over time, expanding the narrative. But equally important is the connectivity between places. This is why the application of Songlines principles as a foundation for placemaking or even wayfinding through a city is worthy of exploration. These enduring principles from ancient times have a lot to offer.

It is more than just remembering. Walking through a site becomes a repetitive yet quiet ceremonial act. Watching the film of Frank Gurrmanamana from Djunawunya in Arnhem Land speaking and singing to a fish trap as he was making it (see Chapter 2) opened me up to the idea of new and more intimate relationships with the spaces and places we use every day.

We have 'environmental corridors' and 'cultural trails', but Songlines as a basis for connecting sites across a city or regional area are a combination of the two. They can also connect a place today with history spanning some 65,000 years, so that the narratives we engage with are enduring and ultimately more meaningful. They can rechoreograph how people move through space over time and, most importantly, their connection to that space. Connectivity is about connecting people to people, but it's also about linking people to place and time, and our pasts to our futures.

149

DESIGNING WITH COUNTRY

The devastating impact of colonisation, with its disruption to Aboriginal landscape, people and cultural practices, has over time created a collective amnesia regarding this history. However, the large gaps in memory can be restitched together if dormant Country can be reactivated.

– Dillon Kombumerri, Principal Architect, Office of the Government Architect NSW[19]

It's probably thanks to the now widely practised Welcome to Country that the word 'Country' (with a capital C) has become so much more common in the Australian vernacular. Since the land rights movement of the 1970s, the Aboriginal connection to Country (or, as it was known in those days, 'the land') has been a well-worn phrase but its true meaning hasn't been fully comprehended: that it only referred to the land is a case in point. It is a different story today, with the land, sea and sky now part of the multidimensional understanding. This is what happens when the collective consciousness moves beyond the superficial protocols of the Welcome: a dialogue opens up that starts to dig deeper into the spiritual beliefs and philosophies of Indigenous people.

The next logical development in the conversation is how this unique ecological and cultural view of nature can positively affect different industries in Australia. Bruce Pascoe's research as part of his book *Dark Emu* and its influence on the future of farming and food production, Margo and Lynne's research in *Songlines* and how it could improve education and neuroscience, and Bill Gammage's and Victor Steffensen's research on firestick farming in the management of the land are expanding conversations in Australia and providing opportunities for environmental, social and economic impacts.

One critical discussion is being led by Dillon Kombumerri, whose work at the office of the Government Architect NSW is leading to a regulation that all new infrastructure developments in New South Wales integrate 'Country'.

This immediately presents a conundrum. What is Country? And how can the average project manager get their head around this concept in order to bring ideas of Country to their project successfully? In some ways the environmental design movement faced similar problems when it began, but through the work of specialist design firms and broader education, the environment has become a ubiquitous consideration for developers and consideration of it is now just part of the process.

Dillon and his team started with a discussion paper called *Designing with Country*, which aims to generate conversations and feedback to help enable future development in New South Wales to be designed with and connected to Country. The paper starts with Dr Danièle Hromek's definition:

> Country soars high into the atmosphere, deep into the planet crust and far into the oceans. Country incorporates both the tangible and the intangible, for instance, all the knowledges and cultural practices associated with land. People are part of Country, and their/our identity is derived in a large way in relation to Country.

151

Their/our belonging, nurturing and reciprocal relationships come through our connection to Country. In this way Country is key to our health and wellbeing.

So caring for Country is not only caring for land, it is caring for themselves/ourselves. Country holds everything, including spaces and places. Spaces and places, even those in urban centres, are thus full of Country, and therefore need appropriate cultural care to ensure healthy landscapes.[20]

Connecting with Country is a framework to guide and support practitioners in responding to this new direction in planning policy in New South Wales by employing a Country-focused design approach, as opposed to a purely human-centred approach – that is, considering ecological systems that include people, animals, resources and plants equally. The team's research proposes three essential elements of designing with Country – nature, people and design – through an architecture informed by passive environmental design principles and biophilic design that explores the intimate relationship between people and the environment. They suggest that 'this relationship could be understood as a genesis for Indigenous architecture'.[21] This is where the tyres hit the road and we start to find ways to bring together a very structured contemporary architecture and construction process with aspects of traditional knowledge.

One of the first projects that Kevin O'Brien, Dillon and I did together at Merrima Design was an extension for the hospital at Wilcannia, which we started in the late 1990s. The hospital was attached to an 1879 stone building designed by Cyril Blacket that had turned its back on the river where it was located. The community consultation process was led by an incorporated body consisting of Barkandji elders who wanted to bring a holistic cultural approach to health and wellbeing. For them, this meant connecting the building to the river. They spoke about the building as if it were a manifestation of their ancestral totem, Pardi the river cod. The hospital is the artefact informed by nature and also a mnemonic for the Barkandji people who, through their empowered process of design, are as connected to it as they are to the river. Dillon and Kevin were careful not to be too literal in their interpretation of the narrative, which was important in terms of making functional and aesthetic spaces. They wanted to pay homage to the role of the totem in the connection to the river and the health and wellbeing of the people using the building, but they didn't want to end up with a big cod!

So, the architecture was inspired by the ancestral totem: walls became skins and windows were the gills of the fish. The building also employed passive environmental design principles to great effect. An elegant shed was made with stabilised-earth bricks, and lightweight materials allowed cross-ventilation in the treatment rooms. Years later, this early work from Merrima Design holds up as an excellent example of biophilic design. It was designed with Country for a health outcome – not just in its physical structure but in the process, which was consistent with cultural ways of working.

One of the most successful negotiations between the cultural needs of the community and the health requirements of the hospital was the resolution of the mortuary (see Figure 25). The community wanted this room to be located far away from where people were

FIGURE 25: Wilcannia Hospital extension, showing the mourning courtyard and entrance to the mortuary.

sleeping, but the Health Department required it to be integrated into the building. The solution was to create a separate pavilion linked by a common roof so that there was a clear breezeway between the mortuary and the main accommodation. A campground was provided around the pavilion where communities could stay for months on end to conduct 'sorry business'.

These ideas have been exercised by Indigenous architects all over the world for decades but are now gaining an increasingly engaged audience. In 2018, Canada entered its first-ever Aboriginal-led entry into the Venice Biennale of Architecture: a multimedia exploration of the connections between architecture, people, cultural storytelling and nature. First Nations architect Douglas Cardinal, from Blackfoot, Red Deer, Alberta, led the installation, which included the voices of eighteen prominent Indigenous architects and designers from across North America. Cardinal said:

> I firmly believe that the Indigenous world view, which has always sought this balance between nature, culture and technology, is the path that humanity must rediscover and adopt for our future. The teachings of the elders are not the teachings of the past. They are the teachings of the future.[22]

This point raised by Cardinal is key, and the reason that the audience is building. Tapping into the traditional knowledges of Indigenous people to inform sustainable solutions to the world's global challenges is in the zeitgeist. Gerald McMaster, a Plains Cree member of the Siksika First Nation, Alberta, and a contributor to the exhibition, said, 'A new critical dialogue is emerging among Indigenous artists and architects, such as the value of traditional knowledge in the face of hyper-capitalism, solidarity between Indigenous peoples, and a search for strategies of decolonization.'[23]

We have entered some of the most uncertain times in recent history, with catastrophic climate-change fire seasons and a global pandemic that is resetting the way we arrange ourselves culturally and environmentally. We have an opportunity to recalibrate our relationship with nature and listen to new voices – the voices of the First Peoples and the voice of Country.

8

CONTEMPORARY INDIGENOUS ARCHITECTURE AND DESIGN

INDIGENOUS DESIGN PRINCIPLES

ALISON PAGE

To map the origin of the Australian design tradition is to track the oldest artefacts found on this continent, which are getting older the deeper we dig. What we uncover is an insight not just into the life of Indigenous people and their material culture but into their design practice. By examining the artefacts in the cultural contexts, we can start to distil a basic set of design principles that are common in the objects, which becomes a framework for decisions we make for new designs.

Functional sophistication

As Paul has shown throughout this book, there are many great Aboriginal inventions, and the common denominator is that they reveal ingenuity. Functional sophistication is the first design principle. Great designs work and work well in order to be enduring, but there is a particular cleverness and lateral thinking in these Indigenous creations.

For example, the woomera is a multifunctional tool that was not only a highly effective spearthrower because it substantially improved the velocity of the spear, but also used for carrying plants and seeds. Most woomeras had a stone edge for cutting up game or other food and wood. It was the original Swiss Army knife.

Notwithstanding the fish traps in Brewarrina (see Chapter 4), which are my favourite Aboriginal invention of all time, one of the smartest designs I have seen is a traditional raft from the Bardi community of north-west Western Australia that is used for hunting dugong. Called a *kalwa*, it is a double raft, made from mangrove wood, with two fan-shaped sections, one smaller than the other, which overlap in the centre (see Figure 26). The wider ends of the tapered sections provide stability at the bow and stern of the raft, which suits the strong tides and rips that the Kimberley is renowned for. Increased stability comes from the mangrove wood, which provides extra buoyancy. The clever part is how the smaller section is unlatched and tied to the dugong once it is caught. The dugong then swims around towing the raft, until the animal tires out and can be drowned. That is a practical design!

FIGURE 26: Side view and plan of the *kalwa* raft, a traditional watercraft from the Bardi community of the north-west of Western Australia.

It is worth noting that functionality takes on a different meaning in cultural terms. Art enhances efficacy and so is not considered decoration but a must-have.

Environmental sustainability

The second guiding principle for Indigenous design is environmental sustainability, which is a tenet of caring for Country. While the materials in traditional structures and artefacts are harvested from organic matter and as such are inherently sustainable, in a contemporary context this needs to be made more explicit. The permanence of contemporary Indigenous architecture requires a more deliberate response to passive environmental design – a sustainable building standard that uses renewable sources of energy, such as solar and wind, to provide a comfortable level of ventilation, heating and cooling.

In designing the Casino Aboriginal Medical Service in the Northern Rivers area of New South Wales, Kevin O'Brien's concept was to arrange the building around a central courtyard that allows for plenty of daylight and access to fresh air. Room panels with a reflective foil externally seal the masonry perimeter of insulated concrete panels and brick. Double-glazed curtain walls to the street, a skylight and courtyard maximise natural light, while keeping the building cool. The courtyard has a native garden, which has the added benefit of providing respite for medical staff.

Another dimension to the sustainability of Indigenous designs is the inherent preciousness of the object or design because of its increased meaning. Imbuing the object with spirit through its story increases its value to the owner, who will preserve it for longer. It goes against the consumerist 'throwaway' society. The object has life, and that life is valued.

Storytelling

This leads us to the most distinguishing feature of Indigenous design: storytelling. Creation stories that are carved, painted or etched onto objects or injected during their making are multilayered and have a distinct function. The stories of the objects' materials and their relationships to ancestral totems, the stories of Country and how to care for it, the stories about ceremony and its role in maintaining culture through strong community relationships – these are the stories the world needs to hear. Margo Neale told me about a community in Leonora, Western Australia, who painted Dreaming stories on toilet blocks and other public buildings to deter vandalism (it worked).

The story and the art that represents it have a function that in turn imbues an object with preciousness, which makes it more sustainable. So all of the design principles – functionality, sustainability, storytelling – are interrelated and work together to define Indigenous design. More importantly, they are a blueprint for the creation of new artefacts, new ceremonial grounds and new architecture and engineering to produce a dynamic Australian design that will last perhaps another 65,000 years.

A NEW INDIGENOUS ARCHITECTURE

One of the first jobs I had at Merrima Design in 1998 was to write a chapter on contemporary Aboriginal architecture for the *Oxford Companion to Aboriginal Art and Culture*, co-edited by Margo Neale. Some twenty years later, it's a privilege to reflect on how far the practice has come, especially remembering my early conversations with Kevin and Dillon. All three of us at various times had been to see architect Douglas Cardinal's work in North America and observed how he translated his cultural values into practice, in particular the human connection to the natural environment. The National Museum of the American Indian in Washington, DC, is a classic example of this. The longhouses and tepees of Native American peoples have also influenced contemporary expressions of Indigenous architecture.

We studied Paul Memmott's work on traditional architecture and wondered how this architecture could be translated into contemporary forms. It was my view then, and still is, that the ephemeral structures that were designed using readily found organic material were coherent with the climatic conditions of the land. They were flexible and light, and hold the basis of what should inform contemporary Aboriginal architecture – indeed, Australian architecture in general. What defines contemporary Aboriginal architecture is much broader, but making environmentally sensitive structures that are a part of the cultural landscape is a sound starting point. When I read Paul's research all those years ago, I came to believe that 'Buildings were (traditionally) used as a second skin, as living breathing extensions of the body. No matter what form they adopted, they were receptive, flexible, sensitive and constantly renewing.'[1]

When we work with communities, this notion of skin and bone is a means of negotiating the structural requirements of framing and cladding buildings in a way that can tell a story with meaning and importance to the communities. In our early talks at Merrima Design in the late 1990s, we would look at X-ray paintings from Yolŋu Country and use them as inspiration to illustrate how the tangible and the intangible were represented by exposing the bones of a structure, and how it was in the 'spaces in between' that the spirit lived or, in our case, where people moved and energised the building.

At the time there was a preoccupation with establishing Aboriginal cultural centres as a way for communities to promote and preserve their identity, share it with the broader population and create meaningful employment for their young people. Kevin, Dillon and I did many feasibility studies for cultural institutions but hardly any of them were built – largely, I suspect, because the business case didn't stack up. There had been a history of non-Aboriginal architects creating large curved buildings that were inflexible in their design and probably quite expensive to run. It was a chance to flex their design muscle and create an architectural language they thought was Aboriginal. They created expectations (certainly in the eyes of the wider community) that you could make shapes on a page that looked like an Aboriginal painting, add a story to them and call the result Aboriginal architecture.

Those expectations filtered down to us at Merrima, and because we respected community engagement as a fundamental principle, we were often encouraged (because of the precedents) to make totemic representations. However, this approach was simplistic as it was purely surface treatment or a first step in exploring the identity and cultural values of a clan and expressing those things in architectural form. There is nothing wrong with the idea of embedding stories of ancestral totems in a design – the cultural landscape is rich with these representations. I think the problems arose in the design language, which became too literal and the buildings less functional because of the preoccupation with their form. They were also aimed at a tourist market, and there are many examples dotted across the country – for example, the Mowanjum Art & Culture Centre in the Kimberley region of Western Australia, which is designed in the shape of a Wandjina spirit. Aboriginal architect Tara Mallie-Hutchinson, in her review of the Karijini National Park Visitor Centre in the Hamersley Range of Western Australia that was opened in 2001, said that 'the use of totemic representations appeals to the "authentic" and "primitive" concepts of traditional Aboriginal cultures and continues the flawed colonial tradition while reinforcing contemporary touristic expectations'.[2]

Experiencing culture through a showcase in a museum or gallery environment can be limiting, and I began to see the value of spaces and places, interior and exterior, where culture was developed and made, as opposed to making a more functional cultural 'centre'. As Indigenous architecture professor Anoma Pieris says, 'the brief for the cultural centre is inherently problematic ... predicated on the encounter between remote communities and tourists. The projected program frequently mimics colonial institutional practices of collection or exchange.'[3] I remember discussing this with Kevin and Dillon in the early days. We decided that a black box that had modular and movable walls was a much more sophisticated space for experiencing and fostering the development of art and culture: not a place where you saw the finished product, but a highly functional place where the product could be made.

However, there is a commercial imperative that needs to be carefully negotiated in conversations with communities. What does the community want, and how can architects enter into a process of co-creation and empowerment while asserting their craft and responsibility to take the architectural expression in new directions?

Aboriginal artists, when they aren't working on commissions, have generally had the freedom to express their stories in new ways with new materials and make bold statements about social justice. Aboriginal architects and designers, on the other hand, have a client to negotiate with, and often several different stakeholders with varying agendas, values and budget constraints, and so don't have the same autonomy to explore their craft. This situation is exacerbated by the construction process, which quite often compromises the architectural vision.

The only way to meet these challenges is to create a space where the Aboriginal architect can engage in arts practice to explore their philosophy of the built environment. Kevin's groundbreaking work *Finding Country* for the 2012 Venice Biennale broke open the limiting dialogue that Aboriginal architecture found itself in at the time. Conceptualised as an installation and performative art piece about the city of Brisbane, it established Kevin's position as a leading voice in Aboriginal architecture. Through his exploration of Country as a fundamental principle, he removed what he saw as stereotypical expressions of cultural identity. Explaining his approach, he wrote:

> The *Finding Country* Exhibition seeks a pluralist contest between the traditions of Aboriginal space (Country) and European space (property) in Australia. Aboriginal Country is excluded from the Australian city. The city of Brisbane, located on the Aboriginal Country of the Yugura [also spelt Yagara] people, is the common ground of this confrontation.[4]

Kevin took the grid pattern of Brisbane and emptied it by 50 per cent, leaving only significant nodes and connections in the contemporary cultural landscape – a technique he describes as 'one of revelation through removal in contrast to concealment through addition', by which he means revealing new conditions through the 'removal of the city, building, mass or even land title'. He uses architectural expression for clarity of Country, not as a medium to add more (confusing) layers that speak to what Western society thinks our architecture should look like. By expressing the tension between these notions of planning and mapping, Kevin finds his way into Country, and into Aboriginal architecture as an extension of

Country. As he says, 'the ambition is to arrive at a new paradigm that argues for Country as the beginning of the city, thereby countering the current condition of the city as the end of Country'.[5]

At the Biennale, in a powerful expression of the Aboriginal relationship to fire as both destructive and regenerative, Kevin burnt a map of Brisbane. It was a bold gesture that shifted the Indigenous voice from that of humble and quiet to radical and assertive, and it shook up the Australian architecture fraternity and gained international attention. The *Finding Country* project was equally a political statement in that it asserted the empowerment of the Aboriginal architect as the primary voice in finding the cultural origins of the practice of Aboriginal architecture in Australia. Kevin rejects the notion that any building designed for Aboriginal people is Aboriginal architecture, and he argues that an industry around it perpetuates a confinement of cultural expression:

> Aboriginal architecture remains a completely compromised idea and becomes even more vacuous when bound to the 'by' or 'for' definition ... The one definition of Aboriginal architecture that absolutely avoids this trap and leads to the establishment of a genuine Aboriginal architecture industry is one where the architect of the project from beginning to end is an Aboriginal person.[6]

Kevin is attempting to deconstruct Aboriginal architecture (in the contemporary context) and its associated connotations. His work embodies strong cultural values and connection to place but he explores a minimalist design language and, through this counterpoint, creates beautiful and meaningful places for his clients. His design for Archibald Street House in Brisbane's West End is deeply meaningful in terms of the story it embodies. The brief for the house centred on the site's relationship to Mount Coot-tha, an important place for the Yagara people, named after the honey produced by a stingless native bee. The concrete structure is dressed in three layers of insulation to prevent heat gain in the long summer and minimise heat loss in the short winter. A fixed garden bench over a fire pit frames a view of the mountain for those who sit on the bench, and the central void, which also addresses the mountain, contains a beautifully integrated installation by Badtjala artist Fiona Foley.

In his practice, Kevin brings a freedom of expression to the conversation when he sits with a community to co-create a place. He can open up questions of identity and expand the conversation to bring in other stories that relate to traditional knowledge and truth-telling, which is where a much richer representation of identity lies.

Wailwan/Kamilaroi architect Jefa Greenaway, whose practice is based in Melbourne, is likewise strategically making a significant impact on the industry. He was instrumental in creating the International Indigenous Design Charter (IIDC), a set of best practice protocols for working with Indigenous knowledge in commercial design practice. His view is that:

> While such deep knowledge has been communicated over generations within the Indigenous communities of Australia, these valuable insights have rarely been acknowledged, appreciated or deemed to have value today … such understandings have great

currency and can provide the impetus for design inspiration and connectedness.[7]

Jefa's urban and landscape design for Ngarara Place at RMIT University in Melbourne explores his philosophy. The connection to Country is expressed through interpretation of the seven seasons of the Kulin nation: six are mapped in the ground plane and the seventh on the vertical glass facade of the adjacent building. Cultural motifs and symbols endemic to the clans of south-east Australia, along with artwork by Aroha Groves, are etched into the radiating map on the ground. The planting, which featured bush foods and medicinal species, as well as the inclusion of seating and a fire pit emphasise the site as a place of knowledge exchange – an inspiration not just for Jefa's work but for the work of many other practitioners.

Projects I am involved with now have teams that are highly multidisciplinary, which allows for even further exploration and integration of storytelling and traditional knowledge. Ecologists, artists, curators and filmmakers join architects and landscape designers, all Indigenous and all leading the interpretation of placemaking and architecture. In a way, this collective approach is consistent with the integration of places into the network of Songlines, which are expressed in multidimensional ways. Each site, from a quarter-acre block to a large-scale inner-city development, has different needs in terms of the mix of Indigenous people involved, but a project should always start with a conversation between the Indigenous architect and the story of Country.

We can see in the work of Kevin and Jefa that the stories, while they start with the position of the specific site, are part of an expansive cultural mapping process. Kevin also adopts the locational principle (see Chapter 6), which positions his building in relation to the network of Songlines in the surroundings. This broad perspective is necessary in order to overcome colonial confines of property ownership and respect cultural landscapes that have existed for millennia. As designer Danièle Hromek says, 'Edges are defined through knowing Country, walking and experiencing the land, camping in the landscape, rather than lines on a map.'[8]

I could never give you a blueprint for defining Aboriginal architecture, because Aboriginal architecture is a verb, not a noun, and it is in the 'doing' that you understand it. In time, and with more opportunity for expression, our understanding of first knowledges will deepen and their convergence with the contemporary world will lead to new thinking that I could never predict, especially when the process is being led by great minds in the field. The Aboriginal architecture 'industry', if it is healthy, will accommodate many different and upcoming Indigenous voices. They will need time and space to debate and find natural resting places, and I am not sure that the situation will be fixed anytime soon. If your starting point is (as Paul has so beautifully articulated) an architecture that is ephemeral and a secondary element in the cultural landscape, and your destination is 'Aboriginal architecture' in a fixed Western paradigm, then Indigenous practitioners certainly need to define their own ways of working that fulfil their cultural obligations and steer the whole of Australia to a place that at least tries to address some of the issues associated with colonial landscapes.

One of the biggest changes I have seen in over twenty years of practice is an increase in demand for Indigenous architects, landscape architects and urban planners to lead the interpretation of Indigenous notions of land ownership, custodianship, truth-telling and traditional knowledge to create Aboriginal architecture. As I wrote in my article all those years ago, 'Indigenous architecture is not a style but a culturally appropriate process.'[9] But what I would say more emphatically today is that it is a practice that must be driven by Indigenous people at all levels. Thankfully, there is an impressive cohort of voices and practitioners coming through in many different design disciplines. We need more to meet the demands of a nation that is wanting its built environments to be designed with Country in mind. This view is shared by Indigenous architects internationally, with our mentor, Douglas Cardinal, saying, 'It is time that colonial nations acknowledge that it is no longer acceptable for design to be done without us or for us, but by us.'[10] This approach will ultimately determine the Aboriginality and authenticity of architecture.

There is common ground in terms of the values shared by Indigenous architects, in Australia and overseas, but the expressions of these philosophies in built form are diverse. In the same way that the ancestral Dreaming is deposited in the earthly realm in various ways, the ways in which designers and architects choose to manifest their beliefs are in a constant state of flux and will change as rapidly as the climate and the landscape themselves. And so they should.

169

NEW STORIES

'From what I have said of the Natives of New-Holland they may appear to some to be the most wretched people upon Earth, but in reality they are far more happier than we Europeans; ... They live in a Tranquillity which is not disturb'd by the Inequality of Condition: The Earth and sea of their own accord furnishes them with all things necessary for life ...'

– Diary of Lt James Cook, 23 August 1770[11]

I only recently read this profound quote from Lieutenant James Cook, which he wrote the day after he (allegedly) claimed a large part of the east coast of Australia for the British Crown at Possession Island, in what is now Queensland. A series of encounters up the coast of Australia had led him to this understanding of Aboriginal cultural values – in particular, the recognition of our connection to and care for Country and how this way of life made us happy.

I found it surprising, as I am sure most Australians would, that this man from Georgian England kind of 'got' blackfellas. After all, it was a meeting of two very different cultures and knowledge systems without a common language, so the chance of a meeting of minds was near impossible. Our people saw the visitors as ghosts, the reincarnation of ancestral totems who had sailed back from the east in their big canoe: hence the two warriors who met him at Kamay (Botany Bay) yelling, 'Warrawarrawa!' ('These people are dead!')

Perhaps it was when Cook and his men killed twelve female turtles during breeding season on Guugu Yimithirr Country in Cooktown in

Far North Queensland that he realised that our care for Country was so strong. It led to an altercation that was settled by an old man who stood forward and broke the tip off a spear to signal 'weapons down' because blood was never to be spilt on that land. This extraordinary act of governance would have awakened Cook to the reality that the peace and 'tranquillity' were purposeful, rather than random acts of a 'primitive' people. If he had been able to see the agricultural, medicinal, celestial and land management practices of the local people, he may have even concluded that theirs was an advanced culture. But the chances of that kind of conciliation were pretty unlikely.

That is why I appreciate the quote from Cook so much: it myth-busted my notion of this misunderstood figure in Australian history. It is why I inscribed it in bronze at the landing place in Kamay. Nik Lachajczak and I were commissioned to create a new monument at the site that told the story of first contact from the perspective of those on the ship as well as those on the shore. Completed in 2020 on the 250th anniversary of the arrival of HMB *Endeavour*, it was a chance to reimagine the idea of historic monuments, which were being questioned and in some cases pulled down because of the worldwide Black Lives Matter movement. The renewed focus on history finally gave us a voice to tell our story for the first time in monuments of public significance.

Called *The Eyes of the Land and the Sea*, the monument is an abstraction of the ribs of the *Endeavour* and the bones of the Gweagal totem, the whale. Thus it speaks to the different perspectives of those first encounters, providing a conjoined narrative of two very different worldviews. It sits in the tidal zone between ship and shore where the identity of modern Australia lies. I worked very closely with the Gujaga Foundation, the heritage division of the La Perouse Land Council, and we inscribed the ribs with etchings of the plants that naturalists Joseph Banks and Daniel Solander collected in Kamay; we included their language names and other details of the eight days the visitors spent there. This is Australia's true history and it is untold – not just in our history books but also in the places where the encounters happened.

At the same time, I was commissioned to make a film called *The Message*, telling the story of Cook's voyage from the perspective of the people on the shore, from the far south coast of New South Wales all the way up to Possession Island.[12] This kind of project is activating interest in Australia's true history, which is what I think will be the next wave of storytelling. Truth-telling and design, while they won't be the main driver of placemaking, are essential considerations that will lead to new art and architectural interventions that acknowledge the true and sometimes uncomfortable memory of places. The movement to uncover true histories is gaining momentum overseas, with the commissioning of courageous works such as US artist and landscape designer Walter Hood's powerful design for a memorial to slavery as part of the International African American Museum, to be built in 2022 on Gadsden's Wharf in Charleston, South Carolina, where slaves were traded. A pathway to the edge of the water will cut through two reflective tidal pools; when the water recedes, the bodies of slaves will be revealed. Hood's work is beautifully conceived so that with the rhythm of the tides, observers will be reminded to remember and reflect.

In March 2019, *The Guardian* published a map of Australia showing all of the sites where massacres of First Peoples had occurred.[13] When I saw it, I was convinced that public opinion was turning and Australians were finally ready to have mature discussions about our history. I grew up in the era of the 'history wars', when former prime minister John Howard said:

> the 'black armband' view of our past reflects a belief that most Australian history since 1788 has been little more than a disgraceful story of imperialism, exploitation, racism, sexism and other forms of discrimination ... I believe that the balance sheet of our history is one of heroic achievement and that we have achieved much more as a nation of which we can be proud than of which we should be ashamed.[14]

Thankfully, the conversation has moved beyond this denialist view and we are starting to address the truth, which most Australians are ready to hear. It comes off the back of an increasing interest in Aboriginal culture generally, with the 2018 Reconciliation Barometer finding that almost all Australians (90 per cent) believe the relationship between Indigenous and non-Indigenous people is important and that 79 per cent of Australians 'agree that Indigenous people hold a unique and important place in the Australian identity'.[15] With this in mind, architects, designers and artists should be able to engage with these narratives in increasingly bold ways.

As illustrated throughout this book, the traditional knowledges of Indigenous people hold a wealth of stories that can be interpreted in the built environment as well as in the creation of parks and gardens. Another emerging area of importance is the reinterpretation of ceremony as a way of activating place. One of the first times I witnessed a contemporary ceremony of this kind was at La Perouse, on the northern headland of Botany Bay, at dawn in 2000, directed by Rhoda Roberts with members of Bangarra Dance Theatre performing on the sand. A floating canoe was burnt on the water and pushed out to sea as Aboriginal opera singer Deborah Cheetham sang in language. It was a powerful event staged for the Sydney Olympic Games arts and cultural program.

Under Noonuccal Ngugi man Wesley Enoch's direction from 2017 to 2019, the Sydney Festival engaged in the creation of new ceremonies, including a vigil on the day before 'Australia Day' as a way of marking the last day of Aboriginal people living in peace before the First Fleet arrived. The audience is invited to gather around a fire to share in a night of Indigenous music to reflect on Australia's First Nations heritage, its colonial institutions and multicultural migration.

Some other untold stories were celebrated in the 2018 festival, including that of Barangaroo, a strong Cammeraygal woman who was married to Bennelong, the well-known interlocutor between the Eora people and the British. She was a skilful fisher and provided the clan's men with fish. Eora women's control of the food supply would have been essential to their status and self-esteem, and to their power in society. Barangaroo and Bennelong first met the white people on the north shore at Kirribilli in November 1790. This meeting coincided with a massive catch by the colonists of 4000 Australian salmon, hauled up in two nets. Forty fish of 5 pounds [2.3 kilograms] each were sent as a present over to Bennelong's group,[16] which might be what triggered Barangaroo's antagonism towards the British. Bennelong quickly adopted the ways of the colonists, but Barangaroo held firm, refusing to eat their food and standing up for convicts who were being punished. When she was invited to the governor's house for dinner and told to dress appropriately, she turned up naked with a bone in her nose.

Two hundred and twenty-eight years later, the incident of the salmon catch became the inspiration for a large-scale contemporary ceremony at the festival. Curator Emily McDaniel, from the Kalari clan of the Wiradjuri nation, designed the event not only to commemorate this overfishing but also to honour Barangaroo. Audience members were invited to take water from the harbour and create fish-shaped ice sculptures using cast moulds. The sculptures were frozen and then placed on a large canoe (*nawi*) moored at the end of a pontoon. A fire and the warmth of the sun melted the sculptures, symbolising the fish's return to the waters of the harbour. Four Indigenous artists were brought together to design sculptural and sound elements of the ceremony.

At the same festival, another work, *Broken Glass* by Moogahlin Performing Arts, gave voice to the unmarked grave of Maria Lock, an Aboriginal landowner in Sydney's west, at St Bartholomew's Anglican Church and Cemetery, founded in 1841. Set on the grounds, the performance piece culminated in a burial that drew on Aboriginal rites from north-western New South Wales, so that Lock's spirit could be laid to rest.

Heidi Norman, a professor of Australian Aboriginal political history, wrote of the festival events:

> Setting these works on the same lands where actual events played out connects the impact of colonisation on practices that existed for thousands of years to how they contribute to our being Aboriginal today. They help fill the 'great Australian silences' of colonisation and reconnect to people, their practices and their places that existed well before 1788 and have survived the five or so generations since.[17]

Australian history – particularly the history since colonisation – is becoming fertile ground for Aboriginal artists, and it is through their place-based interventions that our knowledge about Country will be deepened and the memory of significant sites never forgotten.

PROCESS, NOT PRODUCT: HOW I LEARNT FROM MY MISTAKES

When I was at university, I asked my mentor Bob Morgan, Professor of Indigenous Education and Research, about the difference between Western thinking and Aboriginal 'ways of knowing'. He told me about making bread. In the Western way, if you follow a recipe with the correct ingredients you end up with a perfectly adequate loaf of bread; to emphasise this, he drew a straight line from A to B. When Indigenous people gather to make bread, it is the jokes and the stories they tell along the way and the relationships they forge that make it taste good; to illustrate this, he drew a snaking line over the top of the straight line, suggesting that it is in the curves that moments of human connectedness happen – a wavy rather than straight line from A to B.

Morgan was an educator and saw this principle as essential for culturally appropriate teaching. I thought about it for many years when I started working with communities, and wondered how it could be expanded and adapted to culturally appropriate delivery of design and architecture. It moves the experience of co-creating with communities beyond the functional and pragmatic to something qualitative and meaningful, but the process can still be quantified and structured in a way that allows it to be delivered in the design and construction process. That is, you schedule in time for conversation and the building of trust between the architect and the community.

Deep listening

Understanding the community-centric culture of my people, it was easy to see how the building of relationships and trust was important. But I learnt very quickly that consultation means different things to different people. In 1999, Dillon and I were engaged to create a minimum-security correctional facility at Brewarrina in north-western New South Wales, at a 26,000-acre (10,500-hectare) farm where inmates could work out on Country and prepare for their release. It was called Yetta Dhinnakkal, meaning 'the right pathway', and was run by Ngemba uncle Les Darcy. We flew to Dubbo from Sydney in the morning and hired a car to drive the rest of the way, which would take about four hours. When we arrived, Uncle Les was waiting for us to start the conversation. The first thing he asked us was how long we had to talk. When we told him we only had the afternoon, he told us to jump back in the car right away and return when we had more time. We sheepishly drove off and I had learnt my first lesson in community engagement, which is that time spent equals respect.

I have worked on so many projects since then that I can reflect on what a rookie mistake that was. Grassroots interaction has many benefits to the creative process, and the more time you spend, the better the result. The IIDC calls it 'Deep Listening', which means ensuring 'respectful, culturally specific, personal engagement behaviours for effective communication and courteous interaction'[18] to make sure the process is inclusive and recognised custodians are actively involved and consulted – not only at the beginning of a project but throughout. This empowers the community to integrate aspects of traditional knowledge into the product and the process itself.

Indigenous-led

For his design of the Koorie Heritage Trust in Melbourne, Jefa Greenaway said, 'the use of Indigenous knowledge brokers acted as a conduit between the Indigenous-led cultural organisation and the design team ... to provide a highly evolved layer of cultural meaning to the project'.[19] Such an approach avoids appropriation of cultural content and builds a sense of ownership in a project, which shifts the role of the architect as master artist to more of a facilitator in co-creation. In much the same way, human-centred design uses a participatory process to brainstorm, conceptualise and implement solutions to design problems.

An increased sense of ownership creates a place by activating it with the people who will ultimately use it. Urban planner Charles Landry says,

> Planners find it easier to think in terms of expenditure on highways, car parks and physical redevelopment schemes rather than on soft infrastructure such as training initiatives for skills enhancement, the encouragement of a lively night-time economy, grants to voluntary organizations to develop social networks or social innovations and the decentralization of powers to build up local capacity and encourage people to have a stake in the running of their neighbourhoods.[20]

The IIDC calls this 'Indigenous led' – that is, ensuring 'Indigenous stakeholders oversee creative development and the design process' as well as self-determination by 'respecting the rights of Indigenous peoples to determine the application of traditional knowledge and representation of their culture in design practice'.[21]

Community-specific

Allowing enough time for engagement can make or break a project, and the time needs to be adjusted according to the community. In 2000, I travelled to one of Australia's most remote communities, Oak Valley in the Great Victoria Desert. I had been asked to convert an old shed into an art room so that the community could paint about the British nuclear tests that had been carried out in the 1950s, just 130 kilometres away at Maralinga. There were only twenty houses in the area, so I felt the need to introduce myself immediately, but not by doorknocking because that would have been awkward. I found the shed and set myself up there to start working on a model for the design of the new art room. A few girls started to come around after day three to ask questions, and soon they took pen to paper to contribute to the design of the shed. After about a week, they started helping me clean up to get ready for the builders, and it was then that some boys came to see what was happening. At this point I realised that most of the adults in the community thought I was the new nurse. How neglectful was this new nurse who was sitting around in a room drawing pictures!

After a week there were ten to fifteen people coming to help out every day, then the builders arrived and we were away. The two girls who had started with me took on a leadership role and drove the design. One of them, Mandy, took my scale drawing of the community from the air, which we had decided to paint on the ground, and informed me that I had no idea how to draw maps. She said it had nothing to do with real distances and that you draw the things that are important big and those that aren't small, and the layout of the houses has to do with kinships. I realised I had nothing to teach this twenty-year-old and gave her and her sisters the paints to create their cultural map on the floor.

I worked there for weeks and there was no way my stay could have been any shorter. One of the aunties started calling me 'Better Homes and Gardens' because the television show was her only touchpoint for what I was doing in Oak Valley. The fact that I was Indigenous helped: they placed me and my mob by drawing a map of Australia and pointing to where Captain Cook came in – yep, that's where I'm from. But there was genuine engagement, which continued when artist and filmmaker Lynette Wallworth arrived to facilitate the curation of a series of paintings about the bombs: it was the first time the community had been given a voice about this part of their history.

Eventually we all sat back and looked at the stunning finished result and were so proud. But the cultural differences between my urban upbringing and their remote lifestyle were so big that I may as well have been from another planet. I was young and green and really had to look to some of the middle-aged community members for guidance around protocols, which were pretty strictly adhered to. The IIDC refers to this as 'community specific' – that is, ensuring 'respect for the diversity of Indigenous culture by acknowledging and following regional cultural understandings'.[22] This is as true for Indigenous practitioners as it is for non-Indigenous practitioners.

In my practice now, I favour formalised consultation, even to the point where I think the groups formed to guide projects, particularly those in architecture and urban development, should be incorporated or be a structured governance arrangement. This empowers the community to take a leadership role and gives its members the respectful time and place (and associated fees) to contribute in a meaningful way. This approach really worked for the development of Wilcannia Hospital, allowing the community to make decisions in a culturally appropriate way, to make and break bread in the time they needed. As Douglas Cardinal says,

181

I believe that architects, engineers and any other professional team serving First Nations communities should be compelled to honour the inherent rights of every individual in the community they are serving by acknowledging their Indigenous model of self-governance and their traditional way of making decisions.[23]

Shared benefits

Another essential detour on the line from A to B is the consideration of social justice issues, which may involve addressing the wrongs of the past by allowing a project to engage in truth-telling. Aboriginal urban planner Timmah Ball says, 'Blak design led by Aboriginal people does matter but it should aspire to engage with social justice issues and empower communities.'[24] It gives Indigenous people a voice in their environment, continuing the culture they have practised for millennia and ultimately helping all Australians to understand more about the places they engage with.

In a practical sense, social justice in design means maximising opportunities for the project to be a vehicle for the economic independence of Indigenous people, including training and employing Indigenous people in the design and construction processes. The IIDC sees this as ensuring 'Indigenous people share in the benefits from the use of their cultural knowledge, especially where it is being commercially applied'.[25] Design becomes an act of power, a way of developing communities by using project budgets to advance the economic positions of the people living in them.

It is easy to see that construction apprenticeships form an important part of the mix, but there are other opportunities too, especially in enhancing local storytelling in a building. This was part of my motivation for starting the National Aboriginal Design Agency (NADA), which brokers partnerships between Aboriginal artists and architects to design custom architectural hardware or integrated designs in buildings. One of the first artists I engaged to work with the agency was Brentyn Lugnan, a talented Gumbaynggirr painter who at the time was the single father of a nine-year-old daughter. The Westpac Tower at Barangaroo was being designed and Brentyn created patterns that were woven into fabrics used on large-scale walls across the site. It was a significant commission for him that led to more work on other projects. He was the principal artist on a range of carpets for Ontera-Milliken called the Water Yuludarla Aboriginal carpet range, which the CEO of the company said was 'one of the most successful product launches in Ontera-Milliken's history'.[26] The relationship Brentyn has with NADA has been transformational for him and his family, not just economically but also in expanding his arts practice.

Respecting Indigenous knowledge

A culturally appropriate relationship also empowers artists as it ensures that the knowledge stays with the owners of the stories. The IIDC calls it acknowledging and respecting 'the rich cultural history of Indigenous knowledge including designs, stories, sustainability and land management, with the understanding that ownership of knowledge must remain with the Indigenous custodians'.[27]

There is a definite tension between the straight line and the wavy line, and as a practitioner you need project managers to be on board with this new way of working from the beginning; otherwise, you will spend the whole time fighting for the right way of working. It can't be done without that additional time or without the will to empower governance structures and training and skills development. While that may cost a little more, you are delivering more than bricks and mortar. It is good to be destination focused, especially in project-based work, but it is also important to understand that outcomes can occur from the start to the end of any successful project. After all, it is the jokes and stories you tell along the way and the relationships you forge that last.

ANCIENT STORIES AND CONTEMPORARY INDIGENOUS DESIGN

For the Kaantju people from Coen on the east Cape York Peninsula, the word *piinpi* refers to the changes of the seasons and the regeneration of Country. It's also the name of a 2021 travelling exhibition by Indigenous curator and Kaantju woman Shonae Hobson. The exhibition showcases the best of Indigenous fashion, including works by designers Grace Lillian Lee, Lyn-Al Young, Maree Clark, Lisa Waup x Verner and Hope Vale Arts & Culture Centre, and builds on a year when there was unprecedented interest in Indigenous fashion, with the inaugural Indigenous Fashion Design Awards broadcast on free-to-air television in 2020.

In 2019, a group of seventeen female artists from the Bábbarra Women's Centre in Maningrida in Arnhem Land created thirty-three intricate textiles called *Jarracharra*, a word from the Burarra language that describes the powerful cold wind that arrives at the start of the dry season. It is a time when the water dries up and food is in abundance. This story, translated to fabrics, was exhibited at the Australian Embassy in Paris in December that year and received worldwide attention for the minimalist and elegant patterns of Country. This is wearing your art on your sleeve! The designers, who are gaining international attention, are a legacy of Indigenous artists such as Lenore Dembski Paperbark Woman, Bronwyn Bancroft, and John Moriarty at Balarinji, who started branching out into design and fashion in the 1980s.

Jimmy Pike was born in the early 1940s near Jila Japingka, a major waterhole about 400 kilometres south of Fitzroy Crossing in the Great Sandy Desert. His family were some of the last people to walk out of the desert and settle at Cherrabun station in the Kimberley region, and he quickly translated his spiritually potent stories into art using alternative materials and techniques such as lino printing and felt-tip pens. The boldness and vibrancy of his designs were highly suited to textiles and rugs, and so Desert Designs was born.

The ingredients of success

Throughout the 1980s and 90s, examples of Indigenous design in various disciplines – interiors, fashion, jewellery, furniture – would pop up intermittently. While they gained some attention, they never really made as big a splash as they should have. I believe this was due to a number of factors.

One of the main drivers for success in the commercial space is a willing market, and it has taken a while for interest in our cultural products to grow in Australia and overseas. While Aboriginal art enjoyed success at the high-end of the international art market in the 1990s and 2000s, our culture was generally not visible to the local population and they were not ready to buy garments or products that told deep and rich stories about this country's First Peoples. Timing is critical: the world needed to be ready to hear (and wear) the stories.

For artists, it is also important to think about stories that are appropriate for wide consumption and have a universal touchpoint. When I designed a range of jewellery for Mondial Pink Diamond Atelier called 'Diamond-Dreaming' in 2006, I applied stories to the pieces that spoke to human connections – for example, *Wumura* (to fly) earrings that reference the flight of a boomerang, which you might give to someone who is going away, to make sure they return home.[28] It is incumbent on art centres and design collaborators to discuss which stories are appropriate for their audiences.

Another factor, which I only discovered when I started working with larger companies, was people's fear of being perceived to be exploiting Aboriginal artists. Some of the first 'Aboriginal' designs were appropriated and the artists basically ripped off. For example, the design of the original Australian one-dollar note in 1964 incorporated David Malangi Daymirringu's painting *Mortuary Feast of Gurrmirringu, the Great Ancestral Hunter* without permission. While the designer, Gordon Andrews, probably selected the work for both its homage to Indigenous Australians and its composition and aesthetic, the process by which it was procured and its subject matter were entirely inappropriate. After the Adelaide *Advertiser* revealed the breach of copyright in February 1966, Malangi was eventually located by the Reserve Bank of Australia. The bank said it would 'acknowledge' his contribution but also that 'Malangi's role is not comparable with that of any other artist concerned in the design of the new notes'. It stated that this would stop them from 'making an appropriate payment to him'. Becoming known as 'Dollar Dave', Malangi was given $1000, a medallion and a fishing kit.[29]

There also has to be parity between the political status of Indigenous people and the recognition of the value of their culture and its place in the national identity. A plethora of souvenirs were made for the 1956 Melbourne Olympics as Australia wanted to present its national identity to the world. Designers at the time recognised the unique value of Aboriginal culture and so created postcards, greeting cards, stamps and tea towels featuring Aboriginal iconography. Yet it would be another eleven years until Australians voted overwhelmingly to amend the Constitution to include Aboriginal people in the census and allow the Commonwealth to create laws for them.

This is why appropriate reference to a culture cannot be separated from the political context of that culture within broader society. On a practical level, designers and their clients need to follow culturally appropriate processes to obtain consent from individual artists and community groups that lay claim to Indigenous intellectual property. Appropriation is still going on. In 2017, French fashion label Chanel released a range of expensive sporting accessories as part of its Spring–Summer pre-collection that included a boomerang made of wood and resin to be sold for A$1914. When American make-up artist and vlogger Jeffree Star posted about the item on his social media, it caused a massive controversy. The item had been created with no engagement with Indigenous people, and Chanel was criticised for cultural appropriation in media all over the world. The company released a statement saying the brand 'is extremely committed to respecting all cultures and regrets that some may have felt offended'[30] – but it did not remove the item from sale.

Bibi Barba is a successful Aboriginal artist who was born in Roma, a town in the Maranoa district of South West Queensland, and raised in Liverpool, western Sydney. In 2013 she was looking at her work online when she discovered that the Eclipse Hotel in Poland had used two of her paintings as a repeat motif in its design without any consultation or consent. Images from the *Desert Flowers* series were used throughout the 44-room hotel on carpets, walls, soap dishes, chairs and bar tops. Bibi had created the *Desert Flowers* paintings as an act of healing after her marriage broke down. She uploaded them to her website, from where they were taken and used by the designer of the hotel. Bibi contacted the Australian Copyright Agency and Viscopy, which wrote to the hotel's designer to inform her of the infringement of copyright. Bibi offered, as payment for a licence, an exhibition of her work at the hotel, but the designer refused and denied any infringement, defending her actions on the basis that Aboriginal art is thousands of years old and so is not owned by anyone. She and her lawyer also stated that because Bibi's work contains geometric shapes, it is not subject to copyright, and asserted that as the designer had changed the artwork significantly, the design was 'inspired by' rather than an appropriation of Bibi's work. Bibi took the matter to court with the assistance of Aboriginal intellectual property lawyer Terri Janke, not just to assert her own rights but to prevent such a thing from happening to anyone else. She won the case and at the time of writing was awaiting determination of compensation.

The growing national movement that is addressing the issues associated with inappropriate use of Aboriginal designs is thankfully coinciding with increasing interest in Aboriginal design products. We are entering a new era of opportunity where storytelling and art can converge with design and social enterprise. Indigenous people feel a compulsion to preserve their knowledge, and part of that is sharing it more broadly. If we are creating beautiful, functional and sustainable objects that tell a story, then we are expanding our networks of mnemonics and taking our stories to the world. The world is ready to hear these stories. They resonate strongly through art and a sharing of ceremony that has preserved the ritual flow imbued with the energy of 65,000 years of knowledge and culture. We are bringing art, ritual and story into our everyday lives, and into our homes.

ON ENGINEERING SOCIAL SPACE

PAUL MEMMOTT

Jefa Greenaway once phoned me with a question about the design of Federation Square in Melbourne. He wanted to discuss the preferred layout of public toilets to accommodate Aboriginal visitors from remote and rural destinations, and the traditional cultural avoidance protocols that might need to be considered.

I started exploring these cultural principles in the 1980s through seven years of research consultancy with Alice Springs' Tangentyere Council and an eminent Aboriginal teacher/lawman, Wenten Rubuntja.[31] Wenten was Fire Dreaming and the most knowledgeable traditional owner of Alice Springs in terms of its Arrernte cultural landscape and geography, which is dominated by Yeperenye caterpillar and dingo sites. He had been instrumental in negotiating leases for the many town camps of Alice Springs in the 1970s when the government policy of self-determination was introduced, and then was a co-founder of Tangentyere Council, which serviced the camps and provided them with a governance structure. He identified and reinforced a clear sociospatial model by which particular language groups of Central Australia occupied and spoke for each of the nineteen town camps. By the time I was studying this in my social planning work for Tangentyere in the late 1980s, the model was becoming more complex as intertribal marriages increased in Alice Springs.[32]

At the same time, I was undertaking a study of the history of two town camps in Wilcannia on the Barka (also spelt Baaka) or Darling River, known as the Mallee and the Mission, which resulted in my first book.[33] In both places, I prepared detailed genealogies of the residents and their household members in order to determine what sociospatial structures existed and the principles underlying them. Kinship was the dominant one in Wilcannia, while the locational principle dominated in the Alice Springs camps. When I did fieldwork in Wilcannia, most of the residents were residing in Aboriginal rental housing in town that had been allocated to them by officers of the New South Wales Department of Housing who had no clear awareness of cultural practices. They allocated people to vacated houses as they became available on assessment of need or in accordance with the prevailing assimilationist 'salt and pepper' policy (that is, positioning Aboriginal tenants between white households). However, once a prospective resident was allocated a house they often refused to take it, preferring to go to the bottom of the department's waiting list until they could secure a house in the area they wanted, close to a cluster of kinspeople. In this way, an informal process of sociospatial clustering was slowly occurring, inconspicuous to the housing authority, that reflected the social preferences of the Aboriginal residents. I realised the same phenomenon was likely to be taking place in other regional towns where relatively sizeable Aboriginal populations had been moved out of fringe camps.

As I increasingly engaged in assisting Aboriginal agencies to address their self-identified community social problems in the 1990s and early 2000s, I began to notice how certain Indigenous agencies organised their service programs sociospatially according to local traditional principles. In Tennant Creek, the Warumungu still practise many aspects of their traditional kinship and skin systems. Here I have for fifteen years been a consultant to Anyinginyi Health Aboriginal Corporation, which is fully Aboriginal controlled and directed, and in particular its Piliyintiji-Ki Stronger Families department, and have observed how they organise their service delivery environment. Gender avoidance is the dominant sociospatial principle. Their suite of office space is strongly divided into men's and women's zones. Each zone has a large space that is freely accessible to clients for socialising, cooking, washing and planned activities during the morning. In between the zones is a buffer space and a staff meeting space where the men's and women's teams come together with their managers to plan coordinated, albeit spatially separated, initiatives. Interestingly, I was asked to work with the elders to generate particular understandings of the annual initiation ceremonies for use in the business of the corporation. One finding was that the ceremony, enacted over several days, comprised some twenty or so rituals, each of which, through its choreography, provided learning for the initiates of their respective skin relatives and the appropriate behaviour for each initiate in their relationships to the eight categories of classificatory relatives in upper, same and lower generations. This was a school for learning about the skin system. The same happened for sorry-business rituals.

Travelling 500 kilometres east to the Queensland border, we arrive back at the Dugalunji Camp, established in around 2004 by the Indjalandji-Dhidhanu. It was originally installed for the group by the Main Roads Department, with the residential dongas laid out in a grid. But the managing director, Colin Saltmere Pwerle, became dissatisfied with the functionality of the layout and, with the residential group growing to eighty in number, raised funding for an upgrade and revised layout. He was inspired by his knowledge of stock-camp layouts that he'd experienced in the 1970s and 80s as head stockman for predominantly Aboriginal cattle ringers. These in turn reflected the layouts of traditional camps, with divisions into night-time residential zones for married couples, single men and single women, and daytime divisions for men's and women's activities. We see in these examples how Aboriginal people themselves maintain and adapt their social structures in particular ways in different locations.

Contemporary designers need to gain understanding when working in Australia so as to maximise the wellbeing and preferred expressions of sociospatial relations of Indigenous people, and minimise stress caused by uncomfortable juxtaposition of unwanted relationships of avoidance. Working for a client such as Anyinginyi or Myuma is relatively easy as they have clever Aboriginal staff who can translate these principles for a professional designer who engages in culturally in-depth consultation. However, the challenge is far more difficult in large-scale metropolitan public architecture and urban planning, where there are multiple clients from many walks of life.

Recently, I have been leading a skilled research team (anthropologists, architects, sociologists) focusing on aspects of hospital design in Townsville and Mount Isa.[34] The appalling statistics on Aboriginal health have been widely publicised, including high mortality (early death), yet Aboriginal people have very high self-discharge rates from hospitals and often refuse to go to hospital at all, which means that preventative and maintained health care fails. Our research problem is therefore how to make hospital environments more attractive for Aboriginal clients to encourage them to attend, and stay once admitted, and so decrease the risk of early death. Part of the answer is to design comfortable entry, waiting and visitor spaces that are conducive to flexible sociospatial arrangements, and to incorporate other principles, such as connection to Country, through externally oriented planning with views and access to the outside, biophilic design (related to nature) and references to local Aboriginal geography. Understanding Aboriginal relationships with Country and with kinspeople is paramount in the 21st-century Australian design paradigm.

9

THE OFFERING: A NEW AUSTRALIAN DESIGN

ALISON PAGE

Four men and a woman were in camp. In all 69 people lived in the northeast, the hunted remnant of perhaps 700 people two decades before. The camp was led by Mannalargenna. He knew whites killed men and children and stole women, he knew Robinson's party was seeking his though not why, and he knew soldiers were hunting, for the Black Line, the military cordon bent on capturing every surviving Tasmanian, was under way. He knew too that smoke would betray his small band, yet still they fired the land, in the face of death toiling to do what perhaps ten times as many would once have done. Nothing shows so powerfully how crucial land care was. This was no casual burning. It was a mortal duty, a levy on the souls of brave men and women.

– Bill Gammage[1]

Mannalargenna was an elder of the Plangermaireener clan who led the fight against the British settlers, represented by George Robinson, during Tasmania's Black War. His story illustrates a passion for environmental sustainability that Australia is crying out for. He valued the life of Country over his own, and that is what all Australians can gain by listening to the voices of the First Peoples.

Our culture's systems, technologies and social structures were designed with care for the land, sea and sky and the people in them as a guiding principle. It was a holistic ecological order that ensured the survival of untold generations through major climatic changes, and an everyday life that was filled with art, ceremony and storytelling to strengthen the wellbeing and connectedness of the community. Isn't this something we as Australians can all embrace as our identity? A foundation on which we can build a purposeful and inspirational future that is like no other in the world?

Sometimes I think that when this country was colonised, my ancestors buried their systems, technologies and knowledges in the ground, like seeds they were preserving. They distilled thousands of years of trial and error, observation and experimentation into these cultural seeds and designed them to lie dormant, knowing that when Country cried out for them and fires came ravaging through, the seeds would germinate and the time would finally come for them to grow. That time is now.

There is a new awakening fuelled by ecological necessity to redesign our future and the relationship that we as people have with nature and each other. We can design our built environments to be a part of the managed landscapes that formed the basis of First Nations ecology since time immemorial. Our objects, interiors and places can be an extension of the Songlines that crisscross this country in every direction and are a web of knowledge embedded in our everyday lives.

This New Australian Design will improve the wellbeing of people and create places that ultimately mean more to all of us. It will extend Country, not abrogate it, and it should be created with that in mind – because we are *all* connected to Country.

ACKNOWLEDGEMENTS

With much thanks to our production leader at Thames & Hudson Australia, Sally Heath, in constructing our creative space and cajoling us into it!

A big thank you to the current and past support teams in the Aboriginal Environments Research Centre, University of Queensland, including Craig Wardill, Jess Kane, Tim O'Rourke, Richard Foster and Murray Lyons, but especially the multitasking Linda Thomson, who anchored production at the authors' end. Appreciated support and assistance has been received during writing from Roxanne Thomas of Mirndiyan Gununa on Mornington Island; Colin Saltmere, managing director of Myuma in Camooweal; architect Stephanie Smith in Sydney; linguist Erich Round at the University of Queensland; and David Moffat of the International Association for the Study of Traditional Environments (IASTE) in San Francisco. – PM

I would like to acknowledge Alby and Poppy, who sacrificed time with Mummy, and thanks to Nik for holding the fort at work. – AP

IMAGE CREDITS

Figure 1: Photographs by H McLennan, Australian Museum.

Figures 2, 10: Illustrations by Richard Foster; rights held by Paul Memmott.

Figure 3: Illustration by Tim O'Rourke; rights held by Paul Memmott.

Figures 4, 5, 8, 13, 16: Illustrations by Murray Lyons; rights held by Paul Memmott.

Figure 6: Photograph by AA White; illustration by Paul Memmott.

Figure 7: Illustration by Paul Memmott based on archaeological and ethnographic evidence.

Figure 9: Illustration adapted from a surveyed plan and information by RH Mathews.

Figure 11: All illustrations by Walter Roth.

Figure 12: Illustration adapted from Map 16 in FD McCarthy, '"Trade" in Aboriginal Australia, and "Trade" Relationships with Torres Strait, New Guinea and Malaya', *Oceania*, 10(2), 1939, pp. 171–95 (p. 191).

Figure 14: Drawing by Craig Wardill; rights held by Paul Memmott.

Figure 15: Plan by Stephanie Smith; rights held by Stephanie Smith.

Figure 17: Illustration by Craig Wardill, adapted from a photograph by Donald Thomson.

Figures 18, 20: Illustrations by Paul Memmott.

Figure 19: Adapted from Sir Baldwin Spencer & FJ Gillen, *The Arunta: A Study of a Stone Age People*, 2 vols, Macmillan & Co., London, 1927, p. 501.

Figures 21, 22: Photographs by Paul Memmott.

Figures 23, 24: Maps by Paul Memmott.

Figure 25: Photograph by Brett Boardman.

Figure 26: Drawing by David Payne; image courtesy of the Australian National Maritime Museum/Indigenous Programs Unit.

NOTES

1. PERSONAL PERSPECTIVES

1   Robin Boyd, *The Australian Ugliness*, FW Cheshire, Melbourne, 1960.

2   Claire Bowern, 'Chirila: Contemporary and Historical Resources for the Indigenous Languages of Australia', *Language Documentation & Conservation*, 10, 2016, pp. 1–44.

3   Paul Memmott, *Gunyah, Goondie + Wurley: The Aboriginal Architecture of Australia*, University of Queensland Press, St Lucia, 2007.

2. OBJECTS AND SPIRITUALITY: BUILDING ON COUNTRY

1   Deborah Bird Rose, *Nourishing Terrains: Australian Aboriginal Views of Landscape and Wilderness*, Australian Heritage Commission, Canberra, 1996, p. 7.

2   Margo Neale, in *Remains ep 1 mood* (film), Zakpage, 2015, <https://vimeo.com/123895416>.

3   Scott Mitchell, 'Opinion: Return Aboriginal Sacred Objects', *Australian Geographic*, 110, 2012, <australiangeographic.com.au/topics/history-culture/2012/12/opinion-return-aboriginal-sacred-objects/>.

4   F David Peat, *Blackfoot Physics*, Fourth Estate, London, 1995, p. 283.

5   Dr Leroy Little Bear, 'Indigenous Knowledge and Western Science', presentation at Banff Centre, Alberta, Canada, 2015, <youtube.com/watch?v=gJSJ28eEUjI>.

6   Dr Leroy Little Bear.

7   Definition from *Macquarie Dictionary Online*, 2016, Macquarie Dictionary Publishers, an imprint of Pan Macmillan Australia Pty Ltd, <macquariedictionary.com.au>.

8   Philip Jones, *Boomerang: Behind the Australian Icon*, Wakefield Press, Adelaide, 2004.

9   Skin names form part of the Aboriginal kinship system, which classifies all people within an Aboriginal community, whether they are biologically related or not. Non-Aboriginal people can also be given a skin name if they become trusted and respected members of the community. In the Lardil skin system, paired skin types alternate each generation between father and child to form patrilineal lines of descent. Thus, my Kamarangi skin is determined by the skin of my 'adoptive' father, Burrud, whose Buralangi skin follows *his* father's Kamarangi skin. The skin of my children is, in turn, Buralangi.

10 See Paul Memmott, *Lardil Properties of Place: An Ethnological Study of Man–Environment Relations*, PhD thesis, University of Queensland, 1979, p. 214.

11 The interested reader is also referred to Jones's *Boomerang*.

12 AP Elkin, 'Elements of Australian Aboriginal Philosophy', *Oceania*, 40(2), 1969, pp. 85–98; Ronald M Berndt, *Australian Aboriginal Religion*, EJ Brill, Leiden, Netherlands, 1974.

13   See Margo Neale & Lynne Kelly, *Songlines: The Power and Promise,* Thames & Hudson, Melbourne, 2020.

14   Richard Moyle, *Alyawarra Music: Songs and Society in a Central Australian Community*, Australian Institute of Aboriginal Studies, Canberra, 1986, p. 254 (translated).

3.   ON CAMPS, SHELTER AND COUNTRY

1   Much of this chapter is adapted from my prize-winning book *Gunyah, Goondie + Wurley: The Aboriginal Architecture of Australia* (University of Queensland Press, St Lucia, 2007), which has been out of print and unavailable for some years despite ongoing demand. I reproduce edited parts here to introduce readers to the general character of the continent and the design principles of various structures.

2   Note that anthropologists have used (and sometimes still use) 'villages', but this is controversial in the anthropology field. The term 'village' is not well known among Aboriginal people, who instead use 'community' or 'camp'.

3   See *Gunyah, Goondie + Wurley* for more examples of types and forms from Arnhem Land.

4   For example, see John Mathew, *Eaglehawk and Crow: A Study of the Australian Aborigines including an Inquiry into Their Origin and a Survey of Australian Languages*, David Nutt, London, 1899, p. 85.

5   For example, see George Horne & George Aiston, 'Camp and Camp Life', in their *Savage Life in Central Australia*, Macmillan, London, 1924, p. 18.

6   Thomas Worsnop (comp.), *The Prehistoric Arts, Manufactures, Works, Weapons, etc., of the Aborigines of Australia*, CE Bristow, Government Printer, Adelaide, 1897, p. 79.

7   For example, kangaroos, dugong, cycad-palm nuts, bunya-pine nuts, swamp corns, waterlilies, large schools of fish.

8   Cunningham 1824, cited in JG Steele, *Aboriginal Pathways in Southeast Queensland and the Richmond River*, University of Queensland Press, St Lucia, 1984, pp. 99–100. Also see James Backhouse, *A Narrative of a Visit to the Australian Colonies*, Hamilton, Adams, London, 1843, pp. 372–4 on the camps of the Quandamooka people of Moreton Bay.

4.   ENGINEERED STRUCTURES

1   See Paul Memmott, *Gunyah, Goondie + Wurley: The Aboriginal Architecture of Australia*, University of Queensland Press, St Lucia, 2007, Chapter 8.

2   Bobbie Hardy, *West of the Darling*, Jacaranda, Milton, Qld, 1969 and *Lament for the Barkindji*, Rigby, Sydney, 1976, p. 7.

3   Major AJ Boyd, 'Narrative of Capt. G. Pennefather's exploration of the Coen, Archer and Batavia Rivers, and of the Islands on the Western Coast of the Gulf of Carpentaria in 1880', *Proceedings and Transactions of the Royal Geographic Society of Queensland*, XI, 1896, pp. 46–60.

4   Paul Memmott, *Lardil Properties of Place: An Ethnological Study in Man-Environment Relations*, PhD dissertation, University of Queensland, 1979, p. 55.

5   Paul Memmott, *Material Culture of the Wellesley Islands*, Aboriginal and Torres Strait Islander Studies Unit, University of Queensland, St Lucia, 2010.

6   Walter E Roth, *Ethnological Studies among the North-West-Central Queensland Aborigines*, Cambridge University Press, Cambridge, 2010 (originally published 1897), pp. 94–100.

7   Paul Memmott, Richard Hyde & Tim O'Rourke, 'Biomimetic Theory and Building Technology: Aboriginal and Scientific Knowledge of Spinifex Grass', *Architectural Science Review*, 52(2), 2009, pp. 117–25; Paul Memmott, Darren Martin & Nasim Amiralian, 'Nanotechnology and the Dreamtime Knowledge of Spinifex Grass', in Caroline Baillie & Randika Jayasinghe (eds), *Green Composites: Waste and Nature-Based Materials for a Sustainable Future*, 2nd edn, Elsevier, UK, 2017, pp. 181–98.

8   Heidi Pitman & Lynley Wallis, 'The Point of Spinifex: Aboriginal Uses of Spinifex Grasses in Australia', *Ethnobotany Research and Applications*, 10, 2012, pp. 109–31.

9   ARC grant DP0877161 (2008–12), Paul Memmott, Susanne Schmidt, Richard Hyde, Darren Martin & Rod Fensham.

10   Margrit Koettig, *Rising Damp: Aboriginal Structures in Perspective*, MA Qual. thesis, Department of Anthropology, University of Sydney, 1976, p. 6.

11   For example, see Paul Memmott, *Humpy, House and Tin Shed: Aboriginal Settlement History on the Darling River*, Ian Buchan Fell Research Centre, Faculty of Architecture, University of Sydney, 1991.

12   Peter Beveridge, 'On the Aborigines Inhabiting the Great Lacustrine & Riverine Depression of the Lower Murray, Lower Murrumbidgee, Lower Lachlan & Lower Darling', in *Royal Society of New South Wales Journal and Proceedings*, 17, 1884, p. 29.

13   TGH Strehlow, *Songs of Central Australia*, Angus & Robertson, Sydney, 1971 (map). Strehlow uses the spelling Aruabara. My Aboriginal consultant for this site name was Lindsay Bookie.

14   RG Kimber & MA Smith, 'An Aranda Ceremony', in DJ Mulvaney & J Peter White (eds), *Australians to 1788*, Fairfax, Syme & Weldon Associates, Broadway, NSW, 1987, p. 225.

15   Thomson's fieldnotes, Ref.107, 7/10/35; Donald F Thomson, *Arnhem Land: Explorations among an Unknown People*, 1949 (reprinted from *Geographic Journal*, 112, 1948 and 113 and 114, 1949), p. 6.

16   AP Elkin & Catherine and Ronald Berndt, *Art in Arnhem Land*, Cheshire, Melbourne, 1950.

5. MATERIALS

1   Alan N Williams et al., 'Human Refugia in Australia during the Last Glacial Maximum and Terminal Pleistocene: A Geospatial Analysis of the 25–12 ka Australian Archaeological Record', *Journal of Archaeological Science*, 40(12), 2013, pp. 4612–25.

2   Philip Jones, *Ochre and Rust: Artefacts and Encounters on Australian Frontiers*,
     Wakefield Press, Adelaide, 2007, p. 119.

3   Jones, pp. 119, 120.

4   Jones, p. 118.

5   Kim Akerman, '"Missing the Point" or "What to Believe – the Theory or the Data":
     Rationales for the Production of Kimberley Points', *Australian Aboriginal Studies*, 2,
     2008, p. 72.

6   Akerman, p. 75.

7   Again, I am drawing on my old teachers and mentors in the Wellesley Islands. In
     the North Wellesleys, these people were Fred and Maude Jarrar, Kelly and Francis
     Bunbujee, Jackson Jacob, Gully and Cora Peters, Charles Marmies and others of the
     Lardil; and in the South Wellesleys, Darwin and May Moodoonathi, Pat and Sally
     Gabori, and Pluto.

8   Paul Memmott, *The South Wellesley Islands and the Kaiadilt: A History and an Analysis
     of the Significance of the Land and Its People*, unpublished report to Aboriginal Data
     Archive, Department of Architecture, University of Queensland, 1982.

9   Paul Memmott, 'Rainbows, Story Places, and Malkri Sickness in the North
     Wellesleys', *Oceania*, 53, 1982, pp. 163–82.

10   FD McCarthy, '"Trade" in Aboriginal Australia, and "Trade" Relationships with
     Torres Strait, New Guinea and Malaya', *Oceania*, 10(2), 1939, pp. 171–95.

11   Illustration adapted from McCarthy, Map 16, p. 191.

12   Richard M Moyle, *Alyawarra Music: Songs and Society in a Central Australian
     Community*, Australian Institute of Aboriginal Studies, Canberra, 1986, pp. 91–3.

13   I have written a paper with Erich Round and other colleagues about such a process
     of change in the Kaiadilt lands and language, where we have expanded on such an
     occurrence during 800 to 400 years ago. See Paul Memmott et al., 'Fission, Fusion
     and Syncretism: Linguistic and Environmental Changes among the Tangkic People
     of the Southern Gulf of Carpentaria, Northern Australia', in Jean-Christophe
     Verstraete & Diane Hafner (eds), *Land and Language in Cape York Peninsula and the
     Gulf Country*, John Benjamins, Amsterdam, PA, 2016, pp. 105–36.

14   There were many architectural failures in trying to find culturally appropriate design
     approaches. The most successful solutions, from the Aboriginal residents' viewpoint,
     managed to retain the external appearance of a conventional non-Aboriginal person's
     house. This avoided a sense of shame or inferiority associated with getting something
     different from the norm. See Paul Memmott, 'Aboriginal Housing: The State of
     the Art (or the Non-State of the Art)', *Architecture Australia*, June 1988, pp. 34–47;
     Paul Memmott, 'The Development of Aboriginal Housing Standards in Central
     Australia: The Case Study of Tangentyere Council', in Bruce Judd & Peter Bycroft
     (eds), *Evaluating Housing Standards and Performance*, Housing Issues 4, RAIA
     National Education Division, Canberra, 1989, pp. 115–43; Timothy O'Rourke, 'Uses
     of the Vernacular in the Design of Indigenous Housing', *Fabrications*, 30(1), 2020,
     pp. 68–91.

15   See Paul Memmott, *Humpy, House and Tin Shed: Aboriginal Settlement History on the Darling River*, Ian Buchan Fell Research Centre, Faculty of Architecture, University of Sydney, 1991.

16   Stephanie Smith, *The Tin Camp: A Study of Contemporary Aboriginal Architecture in North-Western NSW*, M.Arch. thesis, Department of Architecture, University of Queensland, 1996.

17   Donald F Thomson, 'Notes on Some Primitive Watercraft in Northern Australia', *Man*, 52, January 1952, pp. 1–5.

18   See Donald F Thomson, 'A New Type of Fish Trap from Arnhem Land, Northern Territory of Australia', *Man*, 38, December 1938, pp. 193–8.

19   Catherine Keys, 'Housing Design Principles from a Study of Warlpiri Women's Jilimi', in Paul Memmott & Catherine Chambers (eds), *Take 2: Housing Design in Indigenous Australia*, Royal Australian Institute of Architects, Canberra, 2003, pp. 26–39.

20   Ray Kerkhove & Catherine Keys, 'Australian Settler Bush Huts and Indigenous Bark-Strippers: Origins and Influences', *Queensland Review*, 20(1), 2020, pp. 1–20.

6.   CAMP LAYOUTS AND THE IMPORTANCE OF KINSHIP

1   MJ Meggitt, *Desert People: A Study of the Walbiri Aborigines of Central Australia*, Angus & Robertson, Sydney, 1965, p. 55.

2   For example, Phyllis Kaberry, in *Aboriginal Women: Sacred and Profane* (Routledge, London, 1939, pp. 29, 30), reported for the Forrest River/Wyndham region of north-west Australia that camps of up to 200 people were sociospatially structured according to both kinship and local or sociogeographic organisation. I have summarised scholarly reports on the sizes of large camps in the internal Barkly and upper Georgina basins in the eastern Northern Territory; maximum numbers reported there were 300; see Paul Memmott, *Gunyah, Goondie + Wurley: The Aboriginal Architecture of Australia* (University of Queensland Press, St Lucia, 2007, pp. 112, 334). Nicolas Peterson's *Australian Territorial Organization: A Band Perspective* (Oceania Monograph No. 30, University of Sydney, 1986) is a continent-wide overview of camp sizes.

3   This ethnographic material is partly reviewed by me in 'Social Structure and Use of Space among the Lardil', in Nicolas Peterson & Marcia Langton (eds), *Aborigines, Land and Land Rights*, Australian Institute of Aboriginal Studies, Canberra, 1983.

4   AP Elkin, 'Kinship in South Australia, Part 2', *Oceania*, 9(1), 1938, p. 71.

5   Elkin, pp. 72–3.

6   See Memmott, *Gunyah, Goondie + Wurley*.

7   A patriclan was usually a landholding unit (estate or Country owners).

8   The term 'classificatory' in this chapter refers to the classes generated by the various Aboriginal subsystems (moieties, sections, etc.).

9   Ronald M Berndt & Catherine H Berndt, *The World of the First Australians*, Ure Smith, Sydney, 1964.

10 Adapted from Sir Baldwin Spencer & FJ Gillen, *The Arunta: A Study of a Stone Age People*, 2 vols, Macmillan & Co., London, 1927, p. 501; the original orthography for subsection names has been retained.

11 Noel M Wallace, 'Pitjantjatjara Wiltja or White Man's House?', *Newsletter: Australian Institute of Aboriginal Studies*, new series, 6, 1976, pp. 46–52.

12 RH Mathews, 'Ethnological Notes on the Aboriginal Tribes of New South Wales and Victoria', *Journal and Procedures of the Royal Society of New South Wales*, 38, 1904, pp. 203–381; A Radcliffe Brown, 'Notes on the Social Organization of Australian Tribes, Part II', *Journal of the Royal Anthropological Institute*, 53, 1923, pp. 424–46.

13 Ursula McConnel, 'The Wik-Munkan and Allied Tribes of Cape York Peninsula, NQ, Part 3: Kinship and Marriage', *Oceania*, 4(3), 1934, p. 335.

7. PLACEMAKING IN COUNTRY

1 See Paul Memmott, *Gunyah, Goondie + Wurley: The Aboriginal Architecture of Australia*, University of Queensland Press, St Lucia, 2007, and Paul Memmott, 'On the Kindness of Aboriginal Country, Camp and Shelter', in Suzanne Davies (ed.), *Shelter: On Kindness*, RMIT Gallery, Melbourne, 2009, pp. 13–16.

2 Memmott 2007; Memmott 2009.

3 Adapted from Paul Memmott & Carroll Go-Sam, 'Australian Indigenous Architecture: Its Forms and Evolution', paper presented at the 1999 SAHANZ conference in Launceston and Hobart, p. 237. Reproduced in Paul Memmott & James Davidson 'Exploring a Cross-Cultural Theory of Architecture', *Traditional Dwellings and Settlements Review*, 19(2), 2008, pp. 51–68, <http://iaste.org/category/tdsr/>

4 The case-study material on the Lardil is drawn from Paul Memmott, *Lardil Properties of Place: An Ethnological Study in Man-Environment Relations*, PhD dissertation, University of Queensland, 1979, pp. 182, 456, 469, 470, 490 and 491; revised and published in Paul Memmott, 'Differing Relations to Tradition among Australian Indigenous Homeless People', *Traditional Dwellings and Settlements Review*, 26(2), 2015, pp. 59–72, <http://iaste.org/category/tdsr/>.

5 Dick Roughsey, *Moon and Rainbow: The Autobiography of an Aboriginal*, Reed, Sydney, 1971, p. 16.

6 Dick Roughsey, unpublished draft manuscript of *Moon and Rainbow* and other notes and miscellaneous writings, Fryer Library, University of Queensland, 1971.

7 Roughsey, unpublished draft manuscript of *Moon and Rainbow*.

8 Roughsey, unpublished draft manuscript of *Moon and Rainbow*.

9 Cited in Keys Young Consultants, *Homelessness in the Aboriginal and Torres Strait Islander Context and Its Implication for the Supported Accommodation Assistance Program (SAAP)*, Department of Health and Ageing, Canberra, 1999, p. 26.

10 Compare with Katie Glaskin, 'Anatomies of Relatedness: Considering Personhood in Aboriginal Australia', *American Anthropologist*, 114(2), 2012, p. 297.

11   William H Whyte, *The Social Life of Small Urban Spaces*, Conservation Foundation, Washington, DC, 1980.

12   'What Is Placemaking?', Project for Public Spaces, 2007, <pps.org/article/what-is-placemaking>.

13   Tim Cresswell, *Place: A Short Introduction*, Wiley-Blackwell, Hoboken, NJ, 2004, p. 39.

14   'Our Story', Yerrabingin, 2020, <yerrabingin.com.au/ourstory>.

15   Whyte, p. 52.

16   Michael K Organ & Carol Speechly, 'Illawarra Aborigines: An Introductory History', in Jim Hagan & Andrew Wells (eds), *A History of Wollongong*, University of Wollongong Press, Wollongong, 1997, pp. 7–22.

17   Margo Neale & Lynne Kelly, *Songlines: The Power and Promise*, Thames & Hudson, Melbourne, 2020, p. 42.

18   Neale & Kelly, p. 47.

19   Government Architect NSW, *Designing with Country*, n.d., <governmentarchitect.nsw.gov.au/resources/ga/media/files/ga/discussion-papers/discussion-paper-designing-with-country-2020-06-02.pdf?la=en>.

20   Government Architect NSW, *Designing with Country*.

21   Government Architect NSW, *Designing with Country*.

22   Canadian Museum of History, *Unceded: Voices of the Land*, 3 May 2019 to 28 February 2021, <historymuseum.ca/unceded/>.

23   Canadian Museum of History, *Unceded*.

8.   CONTEMPORARY INDIGENOUS ARCHITECTURE AND DESIGN

1   Alison Page, 'Gurung Gunya: A New Dwelling', in Sylvia Kleinert, Margo Neale & Robyne Bancroft (eds), *The Oxford Companion to Aboriginal Art and Culture*, Oxford University Press, Melbourne, 2000.

2   Tara Mallie & Michael J Ostwald, *Aboriginal Architecture: Merging Concepts from Architecture and Aboriginal Studies*, Swinburne University of Technology / RMIT University, Melbourne, 2009.

3   Anoma Pieris, *Indigenous Cultural Centers and Museums: An Illustrated International Survey*, Rowman & Littlefield, Lanham, MD, 2016, p. 11.

4   *Finding Country* Exhibition, 2012, <findingcountry.com.au/>.

5   Rebecca Kiddle, luugigyoo patrick stewart & Kevin O'Brien, *Our Voices: Indigeneity and Architecture*, ORO Editions, San Francisco, 2018, p. 21.

6   Kiddle, stewart & O'Brien, p. 24.

7   Russell Kennedy, Meghan Kelly, Jefa Greenaway & Brian Martin, *International Indigenous Design Charter*, Deakin University, Geelong, 2018, p. 154, <ico-d.org/database/files/library/International_IDC_book_small_web.pdf>.

8   Danièle Hromek, *The (Re)Indigenisation of Space: Weaving Narratives of Resistance to Embed Nura [Country] in Design*, B.Des. thesis, University of Technology Sydney, 2019, p. 93.

9   Page, p. 423.

10   Quoted in Kiddle, stewart & O'Brien, p. 96.

11   Diary of Lt James Cook, 23 August 1770. See <southseas.nla.gov.au/journals/cock_remarks/092.html>.

12   National Museum of Australia, *The Message: The Story from the Shore*, NMA, n.d., <nma.gov.au/exhibitions/endeavour-voyage/the-message>.

13   Guardian Australia, *The Killing Times*, 4 March 2019 (updated 18 November 2019), <theguardian.com/australia-news/ng-interactive/2019/mar/04/massacre-map-australia-the-killing-times-frontier-wars>.

14   John Howard, *The Liberal Tradition: The Beliefs and Values which Guide the Federal Government*, Sir Robert Menzies Lecture Trust, Melbourne, 1996.

15   Reconciliation Australia, *2018 Australian Reconciliation Barometer*, n.d., p. 5, <reconciliation.org.au/wp-content/uploads/2019/02/ra_2019-barometer-brochure_web.single.page_.pdf>.

16   David Collins, *An Account of the English Colony in New South Wales: With Remarks on the Dispositions, Customs, Manners, &c. of the Native Inhabitants of That Country*, vol. 1, facsimile edn, Libraries Board of South Australia, Adelaide, [1798] 1971, p. 136.

17   Heidi Norman, 'Four Thousand Fish and Broken Glass Connect Sydney's Aboriginal Past to Its Present', *The Conversation*, 16 January 2018.

18   Kennedy et al., p. 16.

19   Kiddle, stewart & O'Brien, p. 162.

20   Charles Landry *The Creative City: A Toolkit for Urban Innovators*, Comedia & Earthscan, Near Stroud, UK, 2000, p. 18.

21   Kennedy et al., p. 10.

22   Kennedy et al., p. 14.

23   Kiddle, stewart & O'Brien, p. 95.

24   Kiddle, stewart & O'Brien, p. 102.

25   Kennedy et al., p. 22.

26   National Aboriginal Design Agency, *Ontera-Milliken Collaboration: Water Yuludarla Carpet Collection* 2017, <nationalaboriginaldesignagency.com.au/portfolio/ontera-collaboration-water-yuludarla/>.

27   Kennedy et al., p. 18.

28   Mondial Pink Diamond Atelier, 'Wumura: Earrings', 2020, <mondial.com.au/collections/diamond-dreaming/products/wumura-earrings>.

29   Stephen Gray, '"Dollar Dave" and the Reserve Bank: A Tale of Art, Theft and Human Rights', *The Conversation*, 22 March 2016.

30   Jenna Clarke, 'Chanel Regrets "Some May Have Felt Offended" at New $1900 Boomerang', *Sydney Morning Herald*, 15 May 2017.

31   See Wenten Rubuntja with Jenny Green, *The Town Grew Up Dancing: The Life and Art of Wenten Rubuntja*, Jukurrpa Books, Alice Springs, 2002.

32 Paul Memmott, 'An Aboriginal Culture of Suburbia', in Sarah Ferber, Chris Healy & Chris McAuliffe (eds), *Beasts of Suburbia: Reinterpreting Cultures in Australian Suburbs*, Melbourne University Press, 1994, pp. 53–75.

33 Paul Memmott, *Humpy, House and Tin Shed: Aboriginal Settlement on the Darling River*, Ian Buchan Fell Research Centre, Faculty of Architecture, University of Sydney, 1991.

34 ARC Project DP160100494, with researchers Paul Memmott, Michele Haynes, Timothy O'Rourke and Bernard Baffour.

9. THE OFFERING: A NEW AUSTRALIAN DESIGN

1 Bill Gammage, *The Biggest Estate on Earth*, Allen & Unwin, Sydney, 2011, pp. 137–8.

FURTHER RESOURCES

BOOKS

Berndt, RM & CH Berndt, *The World of the First Australians*, Ure Smith, Sydney, 1977.

Dawson, James, *Australian Aborigines: The Languages and Customs of Several Tribes of Aborigines in the Western District of Victoria, Australia*, George Robertson, Melbourne, 1881 (AIATSIS facsimile edn, 1981).

Gammage, Bill, *The Biggest Estate on Earth: How Aborigines Made Australia*, Allen & Unwin, Sydney, 2011.

Grant, Elizabeth Kelly Greenop, Albert L Refiti & Daniel J Glenn (eds), *The Handbook of Contemporary Indigenous Architecture*, Springer, Singapore, 2018.

Heppell, M (ed.), *A Black Reality: Aboriginal Camps and Housing in Remote Australia*, Australian Institute of Aboriginal Studies, Canberra, 1979.

Jones, Philip, *Ochre and Rust: Artefacts and Encounters on Australian Frontiers*, Wakefield Press, Adelaide, 2007.

Kennedy, Russell, Meghan Kelly, Jefa Greenaway & Brian Martin, *International Indigenous Design Charter*, Deakin University, Geelong, 2018.

Kiddle, Rebecca, luugigyoo patrick stewart & Kevin O'Brien, *Our Voices: Indigeneity and Architecture*, ORO Editions, San Francisco, 2018.

Kleinert, Sylvia, Margo Neale & Robyne Bancroft (eds), *The Oxford Companion to Aboriginal Art and Culture*, Oxford University Press, Melbourne, 2000.

Landry, Charles, *The Creative City: A Toolkit for Urban Innovators*, Comedia & Earthscan, Near Stroud, UK, 2000.

Malnar, Joy Monice & Frank Vodvarka, *New Architecture on Indigenous Lands*, University of Minnesota Press, Minneapolis, 2013.

Memmott, Paul, *Gunyah, Goondie + Wurley: The Aboriginal Architecture of Australia*, University of Queensland Press, St Lucia, 2007.

Memmott, Paul & Catherine Chambers (eds), *Take 2: Housing Design in Indigenous Australia*, Royal Australian Institute of Architects, Canberra, 2003.

Peat, F David, *Blackfoot Physics*, Fourth Estate, London, 1995.

Pieris, Anoma, Naomi Tootell, Fiona Johnson, Janet McGaw & Rueben Berg, *Indigenous Place: Contemporary Buildings, Landmarks and Places of Significance in South East Australia and Beyond*, Melbourne School of Design, Faculty of Architecture Building and Planning, University of Melbourne, 2014.

Rose, Deborah Bird, *Nourishing Terrains: Australian Aboriginal Views of Landscape and Wilderness*, Australian Heritage Commission, Canberra, 1996.

Smyth, R Brough, *The Aborigines of Victoria: With Notes Relating to the Habits of the Natives of Other Parts of Australia and Tasmania Compiled from Various Sources for the Government of Victoria* (2 volumes), Government Printer, Melbourne, 1876 (facsimile edn published by John Currey, O'Neil, Melbourne, 1972).

Strehlow, TGH, *Songs of Central Australia*, Angus & Robertson, Sydney, 1971.

Wharton, Herb, *Yumba Days*, University of Queensland Press, St Lucia, 1999.

Worsnop, Thomas (comp.), *The Prehistoric Arts, Manufactures, Works, Weapons, etc. of the Aborigines of Australia*, CE Bristow, Government Printer, Adelaide, 1897.

JOURNAL ARTICLES AND BOOK CHAPTERS

Akerman, Kim, '"Missing the Point" or "What to Believe – the Theory or the Data": Rationales for the Production of Kimberley Points', *Australian Aboriginal Studies*, 2, 2008, pp. 70–9.

McCarthy, FD, "'Trade" in Aboriginal Australia, and "Trade" Relationships with Torres Strait, New Guinea and Malaya', *Oceania*, 9(4), 1938, pp. 405–38 (part 1), 10(1), 1939, pp. 80–104 (part 2) and 10(2), 1939, pp. 171–95 (part 3).

Memmott, Paul, 'Aboriginal Signs and Architectural Meanings', *Architectural Theory Review*, 1(2), 1996, pp. 79–100 (part 1) and 2(1), 1997, pp. 38–54 (part 2).

Memmott, Paul & James Davidson, 'Exploring a Cross-Cultural Theory of Architecture', *Traditional Dwellings and Settlements Review*, 19(2), 2008, pp. 51–68.

Memmott, Paul & Joseph Reser, 'Design Concepts and Processes for Public Aboriginal Architecture', *People and Physical Environment Research (PaPER): The Person-Environment and Cultural Heritage Journal of Australia and New Zealand*, 55–56, 2000, pp. 69–86.

Reser, Joseph, 'Values in Bark', *Hemisphere*, 22(10), 1978, pp. 26–35.

Roth, Walter E, 'North Queensland Ethnography: Bulletin No. 16: Huts and Shelters', *Records of the Australian Museum*, 8(1), 1910, pp. 55–66.

Strehlow, TGH, 'Geography and Totemic Landscape in Central Australia: A Functional Study', in Ronald M Berndt (ed.), *Australian Aboriginal Anthropology: Modern Studies in the Social Anthropology of the Australian Aborigines*, University of Western Australia Press for the Australian Institute of Aboriginal Studies, Nedlands, 1970, pp. 92–140.

VIDEOS, FILMS AND WEBSITES

Little Bear, Dr Leroy, 'Indigenous Knowledge and Western Science' (presentation at Banff Centre, Alberta, Canada), YouTube, 14 January 2015, <youtube.com/watch?v=gJSJ28eEUjI>.

Project for Public Spaces: <pps.org>.

INDEX

Page numbers in **bold** refer to figures, tables or captions.

Praise for the First Knowledges series ...

'This beautiful, important series is a gift and a tool. Use it well.'
—Tara June Winch

'An in-depth understanding of Indigenous expertise and achievement across six fields of knowledge.'
—Quentin Bryce

'Australians are yearning for a different approach to land management. Let this series begin the discussion. Let us allow the discussion to develop and deepen.'
—Bruce Pascoe

'These books and this series are part of the process of informing that conversation through the rediscovery and telling of historic truths with contemporary application ... In many ways, each individual book will be an act of intellectual reconciliation.'
—Lynette Russell

The best of both worlds

TITLES IN THE
FIRST KNOWLEDGES SERIES

SONGLINES
Margo Neale & Lynne Kelly
(2020)

DESIGN
Alison Page & Paul Memmott
(2021)

COUNTRY
Bill Gammage & Bruce Pascoe
(2021)

ASTRONOMY
Karlie Noon & Krystal De Napoli
(2022)

PLANTS
Zena Cumpston, Michael-Shawn Fletcher & Lesley Head
(2022)

LAW
Marcia Langton & Aaron Corn
(2023)

Published in conjunction with the National Museum of Australia
and supported by the Australia Council for the Arts.